LITERARY
PHILADELPHIA

THOM NICKELS

LITERARY PHILADELPHIA

A History of Poetry & Prose in the
City of Brotherly Love

THE
History
PRESS

Published by The History Press
Charleston, SC
www.historypress.net

First published 2015

Manufactured in the United States

ISBN 978.1.62619.810.4

Library of Congress Control Number: 2015949276

For William J.D. Jordan

CONTENTS

ACKNOWLEDGEMENTS

Thank you to William Askins, Greg Gillespie, Larry Robin and Joe McClernan.

INTRODUCTION

When balloonist Jean-Paul Blanchard flew over northern Philadelphia and the Delaware River into New Jersey during his historic 1793 flight, the crowd of dignitaries at the liftoff included President George Washington, John Adams and Thomas Jefferson. Tickets for the best "seats" were five dollars. The spectacle, known as America's first flight, attracted the attention of New Yorkers, who hoped that wayward winds would blow Blanchard over their city.

If we were to review Philadelphia's literary terrain in the same way that Blanchard flew over the city, we'd see a patchwork of styles and visions.

Flying over the city's smoky colonial landscape, we'd notice Benjamin Franklin and Thomas Paine and observe both men dutifully printing their pamphlets and creating new works. We'd encounter Charles Brockden Brown, the Quaker writer who published novels and short stories before James Fenimore Cooper came on the scene. In a surprise jolt upward, our balloon might lead us to Dr. Benjamin Rush and then swing low over the head of another pamphleteer, Matthew Carey, who wrote on social topics such as the foolishness of dueling. Our final eighteenth-century stop would be a visit to the home of poet Philip Freneau, a militiaman during the War for Independence who became known as the unrivaled "poet of the Revolution" and regarded by many as the "Father of American Literature."

Philadelphia's literary terrain after the eighteenth century brings us to dark hues inherent in the work of Edgar Allan Poe. Poe was appreciated mainly by the French during his lifetime but generally ignored by his own countrymen while publishing works like "The Raven." Then there was Poe's friend George Lippard, author of *The Killers: A Narrative of Real Life in Philadelphia*, as well as many other works. It was Lippard who wrote of the inhumane conditions at the city's Eastern Penitentiary, comparing it to "a feudal castle of the dark ages" and numbering the outrages committed there as worse than the atrocities committed in France's Bastille. In *The Killers*, Lippard wrote:

> *The difference between Hanging as a punishment, and Solitary Confinement may be summed up in a few words: To hang a man when you can punish his crime, and prevent his again violating the law…is at best a cruel and cowardly punishment. Hanging is a quick, horrible and unnecessary death. Hanging, however, bad as it is, and as much opposed as it is to the Law of Christ and Humanity, is only a murder of the Body. Solitary Confinement is a murder of Body and Soul. It is one of those punishments which man has no right to inflict upon man.*

Lippard shares his Germantown birthplace with Louisa May Alcott, author of *Little Women*, who would leave Philadelphia as a child and move to Boston and then to Concord, Massachusetts, with her family. Alcott wouldn't see Philadelphia again until she traveled through the city on a train while on her way to Washington, D.C., to nurse wounded Civil War soldiers.

A sketch of Chestnut Street. *Courtesy of the Free Library of Philadelphia.*

Far from Germantown, the Chester County–born Bayard Taylor, author of *Joseph and His Friend*, once wrote a fan letter to Charles Dickens asking for his autograph (he got it). As a young man, he traveled through Europe with a friend on six cents a day. He knew Walt Whitman, who would become America's most famous bard, although the two men were occasional literary competitors. Whitman's humble home across the Delaware River in Camden could not compare to Cedarcroft, Taylor's grand Kennett Square estate, although Taylor could not boast, unlike Whitman, that Oscar Wilde had paid him a visit. During that Camden meeting, the two men shared a bottle of Whitman's homebrew of elderberry wine, with Wilde later commenting, "If it had been vinegar, I should have drunk it all the same." When Whitman was not at home on Mickle Street, he spent considerable time in Philadelphia admiring the new city hall, then under construction, or attending an opera at the Academy of Music. Sometimes he would alight from the Delaware River ferry just to loiter near Second and Market Street and mix with the crowds of workers and ragamuffins.

In a piece entitled "Exposition Building—New City Hall—River Trip," Whitman wrote of his impressions of the then under construction city hall at Fifteenth and Market Streets:

> *Returning home, riding down Market street in an open summer car, something detain'd us between Fifteenth and Broad, and I got out to view better the new, three-fifths-built marble edifice, the City Hall, of magnificent proportions—a majestic and lovely show there in the moonlight—flooded all over, facades, myriad silver-white lines and carv'd heads and mouldings, with the soft dazzle—silent, weird, beautiful—well, I know that never when finish'd will that magnificent pile impress one as it impress'd me those fifteen minutes.*

In *Walt Whitman: The Song of Himself*, Jerome Loving writes that Philadelphia's Market Street was where "the bearded poet (his beard was now totally white) was familiar to trolley conductors, shopkeepers, and even bartenders." Whitman, Loving continues, "never tired of being out on the Delaware River, and once in the winter, he claimed, he even hobbled with his cane halfway across it—until the ice looked unreliable." The poet also relished riding the Delaware River ferry and wrote about the experience in *Forney's* newspaper, noting how much the ferrymen and skippers meant to him, as well as the ferry itself, "with its queer scenes—sometimes children suddenly born in the waiting-houses—sometimes a masquerade party, going over at night, with a band of music, dancing and whirling like mad on the board deck, in their fantastic dresses."

In the early twentieth century, there was Agnes Repplier, called "a shy Catholic version of Ralph Waldo Emerson" and "the American Jane Austin." Repplier hobnobbed with Edith Wharton in Boston, introduced Henry James to Philadelphia audiences and conferred with S. Weir Mitchell—physician, writer and author of *A Diplomatic Adventure*—who, like Whitman, spent time helping to nurse wounded Civil War soldiers.

On a contemporary note, novelist Richard Powell's *The Philadelphian* takes us into the city's social caste system. Powell, a member of General Douglas MacArthur's staff during World War II, had the pleasure of seeing *The Philadelphian* become the basis for the 1959 movie *The Philadelphians*, starring Paul Newman, Robert Vaughn and Barbara Rush. The novel's examination of the once-gilded world known as Philadelphia society caused Powell to comment, "You needed more than money or power to win acceptance in Philadelphia. And if you enjoyed the neon glare of gossip columns you had better stay out of Philadelphia, which preferred candlelight." *The Philadelphian*, perhaps more than any other book, presents the mores and customs of the larger part of this great city.

Outside the social register loop, we find African American novelists like William Gardner Smith, once a reporter for the *Pittsburgh Courier* and author of novels like *South Street* and *Anger at Innocence* before he choose the life of an ex-patriot in Paris. In *Anger at Innocence*, Gardner wrote:

> *In South Philadelphia horses still pull the wagons loaded with fruit and vegetables and ice; the vendor still shouts. Any day one can see the pushcarts loaded with bananas coming through, the wizened conductors puffing from the strain. There are many streets so narrow cars cannot drive through; streets still bearing the imprints of the coach paths of another day. There is South Street, the avenue of the Negro ghetto; there is Snyder Avenue, main stem of the Italian and Jewish sections; there is the east section with Poles and delicatessens and Jewish bakeries out of Palestine; there is Grays Ferry with the Irish, where strangers once dared not walk. There is filth such as is rarely seen in a northern American city.*

If, as William Butler Yeats said, "education is not filling a bucket, but lighting a fire," we'd find adequate warmth in the work of Irish writers, especially the gritty landscape of John McIntyre's *Steps Going Down* or in the intrigue and scandal of the work of John O'Hara. There's also the surprising legacy of

Jack Dunphy, a World War II veteran who married Joan McCracken (later Mrs. Bob Fosse) and author of five novels about his childhood after his first published work, *John Fury*, about the life of an Irish immigrant in the early 1900s. The gossipmongers among us might want to inquire how Dunphy later came to be the intimate companion of Truman Capote.

The comic genius of novelist Tom McHale, who burst on the scene with his novel *Principato*, which some critics dubbed an "Italian Portnoy's Irish complaint," sets the stage for McHale's even more bizarrely twisted tale, *Farragan's Retreat*, a book that solidified the author's reputation. Shaun McBride, another Irish scribe, writes about working-class Catholics in a Frankford neighborhood in his novel *Green Grass Grace*. McBride's characters live in row homes filled with monochrome statues of the Virgin Mary lined up like parking meters glittering in the afternoon sun.

No Philadelphia story would be complete without a nod to humorist, playwright and poet Christopher Morley, the Haverford, Pennsylvania native whose 1939 novel, *Kitty Foyle*, irked critics because it dealt with subjects like abortion but later became an Academy Award–winning movie starring Ginger Rogers. Morley lived in the city's Washington Square neighborhood, once the site of the venerable Curtis magazine publishing empire, and had an English G.K. Chesterton style both on the page and when he walked the street wearing a cape, smoking a cigar or twirling a cane.

In his 1949 collection of essays, *The Ironing Board*, Morley had this to say about literary Philadelphia:

> *You know, of course, that the young Philadelphia writers, mostly from Central High School, came to New York and founded publishing houses (The Modern Library) and publicity bravuras (Alec Woollcott) that really moved books to and fro. But the people who stay in Philadelphia are indolent with an enduring idea. All they ever say is, when are you going to write us another* Kitty Foyle? *And now that I have done it, how annoyed they will be.*

Morley had a lot to say about poet Walt Whitman. In *Walt Whitman Miniatures*, his thoughts turned to the Whitman House in Camden:

> *I don't suppose any literary shrine on earth is of more humble and disregarded aspect than Mickle Street. It is a little cobbled byway, grimed with drifting smoke from the railway yards, littered with wind-blown papers and lined with small wooden and brick houses sooted almost to blackness.*

It is curious to think, as one walks along that bumpy brick pavement, that many pilgrims from afar have looked forward to visiting Mickle Street as one of the world's most significant altars. As Chesterton wrote once, "We have not yet begun to get to the beginning of Whitman." But the wayfarer of to-day will find Mickle Street far from impressive.

One writer not to be overlooked is Owen Wister, who grew up amid silver spoons, a physician daddy, a stint at Harvard and first-class boarding schools. Wister wrote his 1901 novel, *The Virginian*, after suffering a nervous breakdown, blinding headaches and hallucinations and after taking a rest cure in the American West, specifically among Wyoming's stark beauty. It was here that the writer found inspiration.

Literary Philadelphia offers a world of inspiration, whether that comes from the historical fiction of Catherine Drinker Brown, the groundbreaking stories of the Far East from the pen of Pearl S. Buck, the massive epics of James Michener, the urban violence of Pete Dexter or the world of circus performers and fire eaters as exemplified in the diverse works of Chester County author Daniel P. Mannix.

Mannix, the author of twenty-five books, was a former circus performer named the Great Zadma and wrote books about big game hunting, the history of torture and the Hellfire Club, of which Benjamin Franklin was a member. Mannix is also a good stepping-off point for an exploration of the world of Philadelphia poets, a vast and complicated scene that has seen extraordinary growth within the last fifteen years. Not only does the city have an official poet laureate elected every two years, but it also has a youth poet laureate, a role that has done much to inspire the appreciation of poetry and reading in the city's public schools.

Chester County–born Ellis Paxson Oberholtzer chronicled *The Literary History of Philadelphia* in 1906, a catalogue of both major and minor writers and poets, including many names that are not highlighted in college English and history classes. Born in 1868, Oberholtzer died at the relatively young age of sixty-eight in 1936, and his *Literary History* would go on to become an archival oddity along the lines of W. Brotherhead's *Forty Years Among the Old Booksellers of Philadelphia*, published by A.P. Brotherhead in 1891.

Oberholtzer profiles colonial poets like Thomas Godfrey Jr.; Benjamin Rush, "writer of the Revolution"; and Matthew Carey, a writer of tracts and pamphlets in the tradition of Paine. Poet Philip Freneau was a friend of Thomas Jefferson who came to Philadelphia from New York to write for the *United States* magazine. About Freneau's poems, Oberholtzer writes that they "were often composed in the shade of a tree," after which the poet would run to his printing office to put them into type:

> *Some are in chains of wedlock bound,*
> *And some are hanged and some*
> *Are drowned.*
> *Some are advanced to ports & places,*
> *And some in pulpits screw their faces;*
> *Some at the bar a living gain,*
> *Perplexing what they should explain.*

Freneau's mysterious death at age eighty in 1832 has an Edgar Allan Poe twist because, as Oberholtzer writes, he was "returning home in a snow storm, got lost, died in a bog."

Oberholtzer's author profiles have a contrarian bent, especially when he writes about Walt Whitman and how the poet's accidental stranding in the city in 1873 became an excuse for him to settle across the Delaware River in Camden. Oberholtzer, obviously no fan of the author of *Leaves of Grass*, seems to relish the fact that most people in Whitman's day considered the poet to be an "odd stick" and that, despite his poetic legacy, much of his genius lay in getting people to take him on as a charity case.

Philadelphia is also proud to have had one of its own, Daniel Hoffman (1923–2013), named U.S. poet laureate in 1973. A winner of numerous poetry awards, Hoffman liked to encourage those afraid of writing poetry to begin the process by practicing writing short poems about something outside themselves, like a curio cabinet or a mahogany desk, to free them from the sometimes limiting world of the personal "I."

While writer Susan Sontag commented that only a city as weird as Philadelphia would have a sculpture of a clothespin in the middle of downtown (Claes Oldenburg's forty-five-foot-tall work erected in 1976), other writers like Agnes Repplier had a more populist view of the city.

"Philadelphia," Repplier wrote in *The Promise of the Bell*, "has a charm which enterprise and immigrant are equally powerless to destroy." The city, she adds, "is a beauty faded with years, and dimmed by neglect," while lying "hidden away in quiet nooks and corners," all this being apparent "to the eye of the artist and the antiquarian." But mostly, it is the old Liberty Bell that used to be carried across the country in "triumphant processions" that gives Philadelphia a special splendor. The bell, of course, with

Independence Hall, circa 1966. *Courtesy Joe Nettis.*

the deepening fissure on its side now calls imperatively for rest; and Independence Hall—a remarkably agreeable example of colonial architecture—is the Mecca of patriotic pilgrims. All the year round they come to look upon the room where the Declaration of Independence was signed, and upon the Bell which rang its message to the land. Today that message rings the knell of the past, and the deathless promise of the future.

The same, of course, might be said of literary Philadelphia.

I
A BAWDY AND UNRULY CITY

Eighteenth-century Philadelphia was a bawdy and unruly place, and when it came to life's pleasures, the city was anything but restrictive. After the Revolutionary War, Philadelphia experienced a scandalous sexual golden age, replete with casual sex in alleys, brothels, taverns and anywhere else that seemed convenient. Many referred to Philadelphia then as "Sin City."

"The nocturnal culture [in Philadelphia] was boisterous and bawdy," writes Richard Godbeer in *Sexual Revolution in Early America*.

> *Sailors, servants of both sexes, laborers, apprentices, and journeymen drank, sang, and brawled; single, married, widowed, deserted, and runaway denizens flirted, groped, and fornicated. The merrymaking often got out of hand: in March 1799 a young man was arrested for being "stripped naked" in the street. Highly visible among these carousing pleasure seekers were women working as prostitutes. Readily available in taverns and brothels or outside in thoroughfares and byways, these "ladies of pleasure," were "so numerous" observed one visitor to the city, that they "flooded the streets at night."*[1]

But the New Republic was living a "dream" that could not last. Freedom from England did not mean the freedom to do anything you wanted to do with your body. The end to these freedoms would come later, but in the meantime, venereal disease—the price of uncontrolled libertine pleasure—was common among city residents. To handle the venereal epidemic, a Frenchman named Moreau de St. Mery ran a bookstore in the city from 1794 to 1798 that offered prophylactics and "cures" for venereal afflictions.[2] Most Philadelphians were oblivious to the dangers of unprotected sex. Bawdy houses were so common that neighbors generally left them alone as long as no trouble came from them. Trouble in a bawdy house often meant fights, noise and gunshots. If a house was too troublesome, neighbors often razed it; however, it was razed not from a sense of moral outrage but for practical reasons.

The mid-eighteenth century also saw the proliferation of erotic almanacs, pamphlets and books. For the first time, the lower classes had access to these materials.

The unbridled atmosphere meant that in 1779, "at least one out of 38 adults was parent of a bastard."[3] These late eighteenth-century freedoms came to a halt in the early 1800s, when the middle classes were able to redefine culture. The new social guidelines required sexual restraint from women, resulting in the isolation of the old pleasure culture.

This emphasis on pleasure went underground. Polite society, in effect, forced prostitutes into the margins of society, and children born out of wedlock were seen more or less as contaminated human beings who were responsible for their own plight. The pretzel logic that defined this system was twisted, indeed, especially when social mores dictated that the average woman could choose between only two lifestyles: chastity and marriage. That didn't leave much wiggle room. If a woman wasn't married and didn't cultivate the "chaste label," she was automatically considered a prostitute. The spiral of rigidity continued when any sex outside of marriage was seen as a form of prostitution. Although punitive measures didn't include public stoning, unmarried pregnant women, for instance, were sent to almshouses while their grown children were put in child labor pools in an attempt to pay their mothers' debts. Unfortunately, the radical Puritanization of the culture devolved even further when diaries and letters documenting Philadelphia's libertine era were trashed or destroyed in bonfires. Godbeer writes:

> As the culture was redefined, female respectability was also redefined. A woman could choose only chastity or marriage, but anything in-between was seen as prostitution. Prostitution in fact covered all non-marital sex, and it wasn't long before Philadelphia adopted a more punitive system: unmarried pregnant women were forced into the almshouse and forced the other children of these women to work to pay off their debts.

ENTERING COLONIAL PHILADELPHIA FROM the area around Valley Forge, most travelers took Swedesford Road, the country's oldest road, no doubt taking the time to freshen up at the White Horse Tavern, established in 1721 in Frazer, which later became the private residence of poet Myrtle L. Berger Swanenburger, who in the 1920s would write the famous poem "Cow Jumped Over the Moon." This mystic country gives rise to hills and a river called Schuylkill that winds its way into the "Greene Country Towne" of William Penn, founder of Pennsylvania and Philadelphia.

Penn, a Quaker convert from Anglicanism, wrote *Some Fruits of Solitude* while spending time in an English prison. Published in 1682, the book would

William Penn. *Courtesy of the Free Library of Philadelphia.*

Statue of William Penn. *Courtesy of Jim Talone.*

influence Robert Louis Stevenson to such a degree that the short story writer was careful to always carry it around in his back pocket.

"Never Marry but for Love," Penn wrote, "but see that thou lov'st what is lovely.[4] If Love be not thy chiefest Motive, thou wilt soon grow weary of a Married State, and stray from thy Promise, to search out Pleasures in forbidden Places."

Because a writer without a printer may be compared to a soldier without a regiment, in colonial Philadelphia, a printer was often a writer, the dual vocation guaranteeing a steady production of books and pamphlets. Despite Benjamin Franklin's great genius, he was not the city's first printer but in fact arrived from Boston after William Bradford had established the earliest printing press in Pennsylvania in 1690. Bradford's tomes were religious in nature and paved the way for the nation's most famous pamphleteer, Thomas Paine, who would come to have a profound influence on the American Revolution in essays like *Common Sense*, his most famous pamphlet, in which he explains the reasons independence from England was necessary.

"If we inquire into the business of a king," Paine wrote in *Common Sense*, "we shall find that in some countries they have none; and after sauntering away their lives without pleasure to themselves or advantage to the nation, withdraw from the scene, and leave their successors to tread the same idle round."

Born in 1737, the largely self-educated Paine worked as a corset maker as a boy while assisting his father in the collection of liquor and tobacco taxes. His marriage in 1760 ended when his wife and child died in childbirth. When the corset business went bust, he set his writing skills to work, arousing considerable controversy with his first political work, a twenty-one-page pamphlet encouraging higher pay for excise officers. The essay's notoriety was the catalyst for his move, in 1774, from England to Philadelphia, where he found employment editing the *Pennsylvania* magazine and where he once again courted editorial controversy, this time by condemning the African slave trade. *Common Sense* advocated a total break with Britain and was praised for its use of plain language and avoidance of Latin words. As a colonial bestseller, 500,000 copies were distributed in just a few months.

It was Paine who coined the (by now) hackneyed phrase, "These are the times that try men's souls," a line that would go on to become the opening salvo of a million typing students. Pain, however, was no armchair philosopher but saddled up regularly in order to travel with the Continental army under General Nathanael Greene. In 1777, Congress appointed him to the post of secretary to the Committee for Foreign Affairs.

Paine's writings were so powerful that they were used to inspire the troops at Valley Forge when, in 1776, General Washington ordered that his pamphlet, *The American Crisis, Number 1*, be read aloud to the men. Yet trouble seemed to follow Paine wherever he went. In 1779, he was expelled from the Committee for Foreign Affairs, although he would later become clerk of the General Assembly of Pennsylvania before making another change: returning to England. Not one to quell a rebellious nature, in England he supported the French Revolution and wrote a pro-revolution book, *The Rights of Man*, which so angered the English that the book was banned and Paine indicted for treason. Imprisoned from 1793 to 1794, he narrowly escaped losing his head at the guillotine.

President Thomas Jefferson invited Paine to return to the United States, but by 1802 his reputation had been ruined. Perceived as "a world-class rabble rouser" at his death in June 1869, the *New York Citizen* wrote that "he had lived long, did some good and much harm." Legacies change, however, and in 1937 the *Times* of London dubbed him the "English Voltaire." Other accolades followed, as many now perceived him to be the original author of the Declaration of Independence, even the "original zinester and first blogger."[5] Philosopher Bertrand Russell, in 1957, wrote, "To our great-grandfathers, he [Paine] seemed a kind of earthly Satan, a subversive infidel rebellious alike against his God and his King."

Russell explains that one of Paine's first friends, Dr. Rush, would have nothing to do with him because of the principles avowed in *The Age of Reason*. Russell writes that Paine couldn't even board a stagecoach without being refused a seat and that there were prohibitions against his voting in elections in the last years of his life. Life got progressively worse for him because he had to deal with accusations of immorality and drunkenness; at his death, he was alone and poor. On his deathbed in 1809, it is said that two clergymen entered his room and tried to convert him when Paine told them, "Let me alone; good morning!" The nation's mythmakers changed this fact and invented a story about an eleventh-hour conversion.[6]

THE MYTH OF BENJAMIN FRANKLIN is probably greater than the myth of Santa Claus, and that's because the Ben Franklin that most schoolchildren know is nothing more than a jovial, benign Kris Kringle—a smiling, kite-flying, granddaddy figure filled with chuckles, winks and wise sayings that sound like they were lifted from the pages of *Readers Digest*.

The undisputed fact, of course, is that Ben Franklin really was a genius with a dark history. Born in Boston in 1706, the tenth son of soap maker

Josiah Franklin and Abiah Folger, Franklin was many things: a printer, inventor, writer, publisher, adventurer and lover, as well as a man of secrets and mystery. His childhood was difficult, with his father marking him early on as "destined" for the clergy, although that plan failed when the cost of divinity school proved prohibitive. Instead, the precocious, troubled boy who liked to read was farmed off to his elder brother, James, then editor and publisher of the *New England Courant.*

James put young Ben to work as a printing hand, so the twelve-year-old was soon diligently working all the time setting type. In the end, the "technical-only" job proved unsatisfying because little Franklin wanted to write for the magazine but knew his brother would never allow a lowly print assistant, much less his younger brother, to become a contributor. Ben, undeterred, went on to invent a nom de plume, Silence Dogwood, supposedly an anonymous female writer who penned letters to the editor criticizing the treatment of women in the colonies. Unaware of his younger brother's duplicity, James published Dogwood's letters in the *Courant,* and they became quite famous—on the order of a colonial version of "Dear Abby." Soon, everyone in town wanted to know who Silence Dogwood was.

In one letter, Silence riducled Harvard University, an institution for which she had little respect because she believed it had been tainted by corruption:

> *I reflected in my Mind on the extream Folly of those Parents, who, blind to their Childrens Dulness, and insensible of the Solidity of their Skulls, because they think their Purses can afford it, will needs send them to the Temple of Learning, where, for want of a suitable Genius, they learn little more than how to carry themselves handsomely, and enter a Room genteely, (which might as well be acquir'd at a Dancing-School,) and from whence they return, after Abundance of Trouble and Charge, as great Blockheads as ever, only more proud and self-conceited.*

When Ben owned up and confessed to his brother the truth that he was Silence Dogwood, James's reaction was not nice. In fact, it was downright volatile. James became self-righteous and claimed that Franklin had harmed the publication and then proceeded to beat him as if he were a slave. But the teenage Franklin had had enough and found passage to Philadelphia, where he hoped to find a job in printing, arriving with just enough money for a few loaves of bread. On his first day in the city, it is said that he walked the streets soaking wet (it had just rained) and that his "odd" look impressed his future wife, who, serendipitously, happened to catch a quick glimpse of him walking the streets. They would marry years later, after her first marriage failed and after Franklin had established roots working for the *Pennsylvania Gazette*.

The Founding Father's life then takes on a mythic cast. He fathered an illegitimate child named William before his marriage, but after his marriage, tales of his flirtations with other women, especially in France—where the spirit of sexual licentiousness has always seemed to rule with an iron fist—began to circulate. He also embarked on a number of simultaneous careers, including that of inventor. His inventions included the lightning rod for homes and the glass armonia. On one sailing trip, he was the first to discover the warming effects of the Gulf Stream. He also resurrected Silence Dogwood in the form of another pseudonym, Poor Richard or Richard Saunders, when he published the annual *Poor Richard's Almanac*, a chapbook of aphorisms, quotations, reflections, weather reports and other oddities that the public found endearing. In *Poor Richard's Almanac*, we read:

> *Diligence is the mother of good luck.*
> *God gives all things to industry.*
> *Plough deep while sluggards sleep and you shall have corn to sell and to keep.*
> *Work while it is called today for you know not how much you may be hindered tomorrow.*
> *One today is worth two tomorrows*

Noted by some as America's first arms dealer, Ben went to London to work on behalf of the colonies and was for a while the guest of Lord Snowdon, at whose estate in East Wycombe he stayed. Here's where his life takes a mysterious turn. Lord Snowdon was the founder of the Hellfire Club, a secret esoteric society that held meetings and parties underneath the Wycombe estate, where the male members dressed as monks and the women as nuns. The behavior among Hellfire Club members was in perfect alignment with Philadelphia's own Sin City reputation in the eighteenth century, when bawdy houses were common in the city.

In some correspondence, Ben makes references to Wycombe's "underground" life, although the extent of his involvement there is unknown. Ben, after all, was the ultimate PR man. In his book *Benjamin Franklin, Politician: The Mask and the Man* (1996), Francis Jennings wrote: "To begin with, Franklin's Autobiography is about as valid as a campaign speech. It sounds good. Everything he wrote sounds good. Franklin's public life was devoted to public relations, of which he became a preeminent master."

Jolly ol' Ben was a man of passionate appetites. To use a Walt Whitman expression, he contained multitudes—so many "different selves," in fact, that today there are still a number of people who accuse him of being a British spy or of murdering and then burying the corpses of women and children under his old house on Carver Street in London, while others reduce him to a Satanist who worshipped Lucifer in the Hellfire caves at Wycombe. But it was Ben's PR abilities that continue to affect how some biographers see him to the present day. These biographies paint too sweet a portrait of the man, although these portraits are thoroughly in keeping with the touristy imitation of Franklin one sees walking around Independence Hall. If your knowledge of Ben didn't extend beyond this Santa image, you would never know, for instance, that novelist D.H. Lawrence found Franklin "a little pathetic…ridiculous and detestable" and that German sociologist Max Weber summed up Franklin's thinking as a "philosophy of avarice."

Franklin, for instance, called German immigrants "the Refuse of their People," and he referred to the black slaves on American soil as having "a plotting disposition, dark, sullen, malicious, revengeful and cruel."

One evenly balanced biography of Franklin is Carl Van Doren's work that spells out quite literally the fact that when Mrs. Franklin was dying in Philadelphia, her husband was spending his time living it up surrounded by French women in Paris. Van Doren also describes how Franklin and a friend played a prank on a young man in Philadelphia's Oyster Alley and then accidentally burned him to death.[7] Then there was Ben's cynical view of American Indians in western Pennsylvania. It seems that before negotiating a treaty with these Native Americans, Franklin sent them a case of whiskey to "lubricate their compliance."

At his funeral in 1790, twenty thousand people paid tribute to this remarkable human being who was really much more complicated than the fake, glossy image that's become popular today.

At age thirty-nine in 1748, Franklin wrote:

> *Fair Venus calls; her voice obey;*
> *In Beauty's arms spend night and day*
> *The joys of love all joys excell*
> *And loving's certainly doing well.*

Life for Ben was all about the next conquest, be it political, a new scientific invention or a woman's "resistance."

KNOWN TO FRANKLIN WAS novelist Charles Brockden Brown, born in 1771 into a Quaker mercantile family. He was the fourth of five brothers. His father, a staunch pacifist, supported the Revolution but refused to bear arms, nor would he agree to take the patriotic oath. For this commitment to conscience, he was interred for eight months. During this troublesome interlude, his family business was attacked by Patriots.

Young Charles was sent to the Philadelphia Friends Latin School and taught by Tory sympathizer Robert Proud, who also wrote a book on the history of Pennsylvania. At age fifteen, he knew Benjamin Franklin well enough that he was able to meet in the latter's house after establishing the Belles Lettres Club with eight male friends. The teenage group took on such philosophical issues as the morality of suicide, questioning whether there was ever a rationalization for lying and the limits of liberty.

According to William Dunlap's 1822 *Memoirs of Charles Brockden Brown, the American Novelist*, the physically frail Brown—who had invented a unique style of shorthand to take notes in class—had a physical breakdown while attending school. The cause was attributed to too much study. The Brown family insisted that young Charles become a lawyer, so the future novelist spent six years in a law firm before realizing that the law was not for him. To escape additional family pressure, Charles packed his bags and headed for New York. The year was 1793. About lawyering, Brown said, "I was perpetually encumbered with the rubbish of the law."

In New York, he joined the Friendly Club, an intellectual discussion group. He became friends with the club's founder, Elihu Hubbard Smith, a physician and man of letters who encouraged him to resist family pressure to give up his literary projects and return to Philadelphia to work in the family business.

The years between 1793 and 1798 were a time of intense writing for Brown, although his output tended to be published letters in newspapers. These were the novelist's formative years, when his long-term literary projects never seemed to pan out. It didn't help that the young writer—who would go on to be known as the greatest American novelist before James Fenimore Cooper—was suffering from a kind of existential malaise, a condition that disappeared somewhat when he became editor of the *Monthly Magazine and American Review*, the official magazine of the Friendly Club.

In 1798, Brown shared a New York apartment with Smith and William Johnson, a lawyer. "Brown was without system in everything," Dunlap writes about this period in the writer's life. "He was negligent of personal appearance, even to slovenliness; while Smith was in cleanliness, neatness and attention to the proprieties of dress, a perfect model."

The men's happy domicile would change when cases of yellow fever began to break out in New York. Smith contracted the disease and died while caring for patients, while Brown himself became seriously ill but survived, although the pestilence had left its mark on him.

Dunlap writes that while "Brown's symptoms yielded to medicine, not so his friend's; he lingered a few days in a state allied to stupor; the efforts of his medical friends Miller and Mitchell were utterly unavailing; he saw the last symptom of disease, black vomit, pronounced the word 'decomposition,' and died."

In a letter to his brother James in 1798, Brown wrote:

> *This pestilential air seems to be extending itself to all quarters. Things here wear a very gloomy aspect. Pearl and Water Streets are wholly desolate, and all business is at a standstill. The lowest computation supposes one-half of the inhabitants to have fled. Notwithstanding this depopulation, especially in the most infected spots, I'm sorry to add that the malignity increases, and the number of deaths.*

In another letter to his brother, Brown writes, "When calamity is at a distance it affects us but little, and no sympathy for others to realize that distress which does not immediately affect us."

It was the death of his friend Smith that catapulted Brown into a feverish period of novel writing and that set him on a course to become the greatest American novelist before James Fenimore Cooper. In one of his greatest works, *Ormond, or the Secret Witness*, Brown writes:

> *The strongest mind is swayed by circumstances. There is no firmness of integrity, perhaps able to repel every species of temptation, which is produced by the present constitution of human affairs, and yet temptation is successful, chiefly by virtue of its gradual and invisible approaches. We rush into danger, because we are not aware of its existence, and have not therefore provided the means of safety, and the dæmon that seizes us is hourly reinforced by habit. Our opposition grows fainter in proportion as our adversary acquires new strength, and the man becomes enslaved by the most sordid vices, whose fall would, at a former period, have been deemed impossible, or who would have been imagined liable to any species of depravity, more than to this.*

IF THIS WAS A DELICATE TIME for writers in Philadelphia, it was also an experimental time for booksellers, as we learn in A.P. Brotherhead's book *Forty Years Among the Booksellers of Philadelphia*.

Joseph Campbell owned and operated a bookstore at the southwest corner of Sixth and Chestnut Streets in 1849. Brotherhead writes that Campbell's nature "was brusque and fearless" and that he had "the characteristics of his Irish countrymen—acted first and thought afterwards."

Born in England, where he involved himself in unpopular political activities promoting the Chartist movement, Campbell immigrated to the United States, where, according to Brotherhead, "he at once pushed with resistless energy into political and religious disputes, and soon became a marked man among the most violent of extremists."

A popular topic of the day was slavery, and Campbell, being pro-slavery, not only engaged in fierce debates in Franklin Hall at South Sixth Street near Arch but also elaborated his extreme pro-slavery views in a book entitled *Negromania*. The book did not sell, but Campbell went on to publish *Liberty*, in which he praised Robespierre and the French Revolution. A Catholic turned dogmatic atheist, the sometime author and bookseller, so Brotherhead tells us, "died in the faith of the Catholic Church after years of more matured experience." The intervening years, however, saw him moving his bookstore to Fifth and Chestnut and then to the basement of what was then the Bank of Pennsylvania, near the United States Custom House.

Brotherhead explains that in 1861, at the beginning of the Civil War, Campbell's basement store became a gathering place for "hot headed Democrats, who opposed the government in its action in arresting malcontents and opposers of government action."

The issue, of course, was the suspension of habeas corpus. "Many arrests were made," Brotherhead tells us, "and a number of them were imprisoned who became violent in their opposition to the government…Pamphlets were issued from this center, and it became widely known through the country, and gained the sympathy and encouragement of the Copperheads generally."

THE CIVIL WAR WOULD ALSO affect the life and career of writer Louisa May Alcott when she decided, as a young woman, to drop everything and travel to Washington, D.C., to care for dying and injured soldiers.

Born on November 29, 1832, when Louisa was two years old, her family left Philadelphia's Germantown section for Boston, Massachusetts, where they would live on Beacon Hill's Pinckney Street before moving to Concord, Massachusetts, to settle permanently.

The author of *Little Women* came into the world with dark hair, a trait that in the 1840s was considered to have satanic overtones. Louisa's father, Bronson Alcott, and her mother, Abagail May, took note of this fact, so their disappointment in the rebellious Louisa started early on. Bronson, an eccentric and oddly flamboyant figure with his long blond hair, capes and canes, nevertheless became known for his progressive ideas about education: the idea that all children are really angels (the blond ones, anyway) who can teach adults rather than the other way around.

Bronson, whose former name was Amos, grew up in a very poor family. Throughout his life, he had difficulty getting along with people, although his greatest fault, at least among most Alcott biographers, was his inability to make a living and support his family. He was regarded as an educational genius despite the fact that he had only a fifth grade education. Despite his lack of education, he was able to count among his friends the intellectual elite of New England transcendentalists: Ralph Waldo Emerson, Henry David Thoreau and Nathaniel Hawthorne.

Growing up, Louisa was able to visit Emerson's library, take long conversational walks with Thoreau or have occasional chats with Margaret Fuller. "No boy could be my friend till I had beaten him in a race," Alcott wrote, "and no girl if she refused to climb trees, leap fences."

At fifteen years of age, she vowed that she would rectify her family's poverty by doing "something by and by…Don't care what, teach, sew, act, write, anything to keep the family…And I'll be rich and famous and happy before I die, see if I won't!"

To achieve that goal, she began working as a seamstress, governess, teacher and household servant. She also began writing and publishing poetry and short stories for popular magazines. At twenty-two, she published her first book, *Flower Fables*. In 1863, she was working as a volunteer nurse with the Civil War wounded at the Union Hotel Hospital in Washington, D.C. Louisa was one of the first women to join a number of other female nurses who came to the aid of the Civil War wounded, thanks mainly to the efforts of Dorothea Dix, who was able to break the gender barrier when it came to women caring for male patients.[8]

In *Hospital Sketches*, Louisa's published memoir of those nursing years, she writes of her impressions of Philadelphia while en route to Washington, D.C.:

Philadelphia—An old place, full of Dutch women, in "bellus top" bonnets, selling vegetables, in long, open markets. Everyone seems to be scrubbing their white steps, all the houses look like tidy jails. With their outside shutters. Several have crape [sic] on the door-handles, and many have flags flying from roof or balcony. Few men appear, and the women seem to do the business, which, perhaps, accounts for its being so well done. Pass fine buildings, but don't know what they are. Would like to stop and see my native city; for, having left it at the tender age of two, my recollections are not vivid.[9]

While caring for the wounded at the Union Hotel, Louisa became very sick. Unfortunately, one of the methods used to help cure her was mercury, which almost caused her death. The Alcott family brought her back to Concord, where she lost all her hair and remained bedridden for months. She published *Hospital Sketches* when she recovered and then set to work on her novel *Moods*, which was poorly reviewed. Louisa's special affection for *Moods* would last until the end of her life, despite the fact that she revised and republished the book to a second set of bad reviews. She came to write *Little Women* when her publisher suggested that she write a book for little girls. The suggestion annoyed her because she assumed that writing for children was demeaning and not a worthy task for a true novelist. She ignored her publisher's request until her father, at the request of the publisher, pleaded with her to write the book, if only "for him." Finally, Louisa consented. *Little Women* became an instant bestseller and catapulted the author to worldwide fame; the book's heroine, Jo March, became as iconic a figure as Huck Finn. During her lifetime, Louisa wrote thirty books and many collections of stories, including some very racy and lurid stories, such as "Pauline's Peril and Punishment," that she published under a pseudonym.

Known as a social reformer, an abolitionist and a crusader for women's rights, Louisa died on March 6, 1888, two days after her father.

Although she never returned to live in Philadelphia, the plaque that stands in front of her family's home in Germantown is for many Philadelphians reason enough to believe that the city played a small part in the formation of this great writer.

WHILE MANY NATIONAL LITERARY figures visited Philadelphia, travel to the City of Brotherly Love may have had little to do with the formation of James Whitcomb Riley. When the poet paid a visit to the Glen Loch (later named

Loch Aerie) mansion in Frazer, Pennsylvania, sometime in 1895 or 1899 during his tours of eastern U.S. cities, Philadelphia's wild decades had long since passed.

Riley visited William E. Lockwood in Glen Loch, Pennsylvania, sometime in 1895 or 1899 and arrived at the Glen Loch station of the Pennsylvania Railroad. That station was nestled nicely in the 836-acre estate of Lockwood, founder of Glen Loch and the millionaire manufacturer of the popular paper collar for men. Riley, at that time, undoubtedly noticed that Lockwood's Italianate Victorian Gothic marble and blue limestone mansion—built from quarries that have long been covered over by Route 202 and designed by architect Addison Hutton with its eaves, torrents, arches, tower and cranberry stained-glass windows—resembled his own Indiana home.

Why the poet chose to visit Lockwood is unclear—unless, of course, the wealthy businessman had an avid desire to host America's most popular poet. Whatever the reason, Riley was now in the most spectacular house in Chester County, Pennsylvania. In those days, the area was filled with grain dealers, dairy farmers, so-called maiden schoolteachers and marble quarries. Glen Loch—Scottish for "lake of the glen"—was Lockwood's personal kingdom, an area rich in Revolutionary War lore. The fields and forests there have long yielded Continental army muskets and cannonballs, which, at least until the 1960s, were occasionally unearthed by children or farmers. It was in these fields and forests that General Washington and his men established camps on their way to Valley Forge. The original 836-acre estate once housed three separate farms, tenant houses and four railroad stations. Glen Loch, in fact, constituted an entire town and had its own post office. The mansion itself cost $250,000 to build. The property also contained a number of springs, which attracted the wandering (and lustful) eye of the Pennsylvania Railroad (PRR).

The PRR had already engaged Lockwood's fury when it built and named the Glen Loch train station without getting his permission to use the name, causing Lockwood to change the name of the estate to Loch Aerie. The PRR would also break its promise to Lockwood that it would maintain the pipes that carried water from the estate's springs for the railroad's upkeep of its steam locomotives. In addition to breaking this contractual agreement, the PRR used all of the water from the estate, leaving the Lockwood family high and dry.

Lockwood had no choice but to fight the PRR, but this would be a battle he would lose. The fight cost him his fortune. When Lockwood died in 1911 at age seventy-nine, he left behind two daughters, Miss Daisy and Miss Edith, and a son, William E. Lockwood Jr., who died in 1949.

"The Hoosier Poet," as Riley was called, was from Indiana, although his family was originally from Pennsylvania. He started his career as a newspaper humorist, but after he began to publish verse, Canadian poet Bliss Carman and literary critic William Dean Howells considered him "the greatest poet of our generation." Among Riley's several trips to Philadelphia was the time he was asked to pose for a portrait by Sargent. The poet spent some time at the luxurious Hotel Walton on the southeast corner of Broad and Locust Streets but was constantly losing his way navigating the streets of the city while making his way to and from Sargent's studio, some six blocks distant. In Joyce Kilmer's *New York Times* remembrance of Riley on occasion of the poet's death in July 1916, we learn that Riley was "always immaculately dressed" and that one of his ideas of relaxation, at the Walton and elsewhere, was to stretch out on a bed, shoes off, while enjoying a good tobacco chew. Despite his stature as a major American poet of his day, he thought of himself as an ugly man, and it was not uncommon to hear him utter deprecatory terms when describing himself to others.

II
WORDS AS COMMON CURRENCY

In Brotherhead's *Old Booksellers of Philadelphia*, there are other curious descriptions of old booksellers that probably wouldn't see the light of print today.

About bookseller Apley, who had a shop on Chestnut Street between Sixth and Seventh Streets around 1879, Brotherhead writes:

> *He was a man of about fifty years of age or thereabouts; he might have been older, but his dirty and ragged appearance made it difficult to say how old he was. He always looked dark and sallow. His features were not repulsive to look at, but they had that miserly cast which at one glance caused him to be a marked character. The windows of the store were so thick with dirt and rubbish that is was difficult to see the titles of the books.*

Brotherhead lets loose on a man named Hugh Hamel,

> *who had risen from a mere peddler of books, and by dint of perseverance, collected them as a junk dealer collects his rubbish. He was probably the most ignorant of all the old booksellers in this city. At one time he could not write his own name. He was in appearance a thick-set, low-looking, vulgar Irishman; and it is to be regretted that the latter years of his life were as much devoted to stimulants as to his business.*

In other words, Hamel was a drunk.

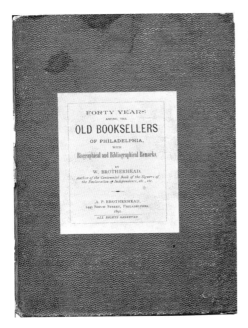

Old Booksellers of Philadelphia. Courtesy of Greg Gillespie.

Bookseller Scanlan was "a clearheaded and conscientious man, an Irishman by birth…an earnest man with very strong Roman Catholic views on religion. Though seemingly tolerant to others who differed with him, below the surface you could see the Catholic of the Middle Ages."

Brotherhead's skeptical view of the Irish is perhaps understandable given the temper of the times. At no point, of course, does he say anything untoward about the English or Scottish booksellers. He tends to keep that professional. He also has little or nothing to write about the writers of the day, including Edgar Allan Poe's friend George Lippard.

NINETEENTH-CENTURY PHILADELPHIA WRITER George Lippard was born in Chester County. He received a haphazard education in a Methodist seminary at fifteen years old in Upstate New York before deciding that he didn't want to be a preacher. Lippard discontinued his studies and headed back to Pennsylvania, but not, as it turns out, to live with his parents, who were very ill—his mother had tuberculosis, and his father was severely crippled—but with his grandfather and two aunts in Germantown.

The young writer-to-be loved the Germantown section of the city and especially the woods around the Wissahickon Creek, so it is likely that much of his time was spent hiking and exploring the area, especially the old Indian trails there. This idyllic interlude was cut short by his father's death in 1837, when Lippard was not given any part of the estate. The empty "last gesture" from his father caused young George to become penniless. Although he would work as a law assistant at various city law firms, the work was sporadic and not enough to support him, so he wound up on the streets of the city, a vagabond, sleeping in the open, in abandoned buildings, under trees or along the banks of the Delaware. His life for a period of

George Lippard. *Courtesy of the Library of Congress.*

time was much like the lives of the aimless drifter types we see standing in front of convenience stores today offering to hold the door for you (for a tip) or the traffic panhandlers who carry cardboard "I am homeless" signs while parading through traffic lanes.

This happened during the depression of 1837–44, but the experience provided Lippard with a sense of how poor people are treated by the very rich and how difficult it is for poor people to "pull themselves up by their own bootstraps" when confronted with the biases and barriers set up by the wealthy ruling class.

Despite these difficulties, Lippard managed to find time to write a novel, *Lady Annabel*, which his friend Poe read and didn't think half bad, despite

Poe's somewhat condescending attitude toward his writer friend.[10] Since writing novels rarely generated a lot of cash, Lippard found a newspaper job at the (Philadelphia-based) *Spirit of the Times* newspaper, where he wrote satirical columns that attacked the rich and other writers. He also did crime reporting, something that appealed to his somewhat lurid imagination, since Philadelphia at the time had passed from its former colonial glory to a much lower status, often described as a "place for murder and intrigue."

Lippard's writing generated a lot of controversy, although he soon became a bestselling novelist, despite the fact that literary critics criticized his work for its gratuitous sensationalism. During his life he cut a daring personal figure because he resembled the young poet Lord Byron, with his thick eyebrows almost connecting above the bridge of his nose and his long straight hair framing an angular face that many were quick to describe as poetically dreamy and good looking. Lippard, in his role as a columnist for the *Spirit*, had plenty to say if only because homelessness had made him aware of the terrible treatment of the down and out in the City of Brotherly Love. This fact set him on a mission: to become a writer "for the masses."

While the so-called master of the macabre Poe may have condescended to Lippard as a "lesser version of himself," many readers today who have had a chance to read Lippard's novels and essays come away with the feeling that "Lippard makes Poe look like Mother Goose." Appreciation for Lippard, in fact, has had a "sleeper" quality to it, unlike Poe's meteoritic rise immediately after his death (he was especially praised and appreciated in France). To this day, Lippard is too often referred to as "Poe's Philadelphia friend," although most critics today see him as an important, complex writer and antebellum novelist.

This is how Lippard describes the area around Sixth and South Streets in 1840 in his novel *The Killers: A Narrative of Real Life in Philadelphia*:

> *Six three story brick houses built upon an area of ground scarcely sufficient for the foundation of one comfortable dwelling. Each of these houses comprised three rooms and a cellar. The cellar and each of the rooms was the abode of the family. And thus, packed within that narrow space, twenty-four families managed to exist, or rather to die by slow torture, within the six houses of Runnel's Court. Whites and blacks, old and young, rumsellers and their customers, were packed together there. Amid noxious smells, rags and filth, as thick and foul as insects in a decaying carcass.*[11]

In Chapter 7 of the same book, Lippard describes a riot on election night in 1849:

> *...Bonfires were blazing in every street, crowds of voters collected around every poll, and every groggery and bar-room packed with drunken men. The entire city and country was astir. And a murmer arose from the city, through the stillness of night, like the tramp of an immense army...Through this district, at an early hour on the night of election, a furniture car, filled with blazing tar barrels, was dragged by a number of men and boys, who yelled like demons, as they whirled their locomotive bonfire through the streets.*

Lippard also wrote of the way Poe was treated during his life in an essay published after his friend's death:

> *One day, news came that the poet was dead. All at once the world found out his greatness. Literary hucksters who had lied about him, booksellers who had left him to starve, gentlemen of literature, who had seen him walk the hot streets of Philadelphia without food or shelter—these all opened their floodgates of eulogy, and slavered with panegyric the man whom living they would have seen die in the next ditch without one effort to save him. This is the joke of the thing.*

In his travels about the city, he loved to wear colorful, flamboyant capes, under which he always carried a dagger or two. He also carried a cane in the shape of a sword and had a belt or brace of loaded pistols around his waist. Such shenanigans today would get him thrown into the back of a police wagon or sent to the psych ward of a mental hospital.

Lippard had no interest in writing for critics or for the upper classes. In addition to writing, he had his eye set on the working-class masses and put his energy into becoming an early labor union organizer, forming the Brotherhood of the Union in 1849, an organization that sought "the unity of all workers." By October 1850, there would be Brotherhood chapters in nineteen states.

As if the formerly homeless writer didn't have enough to do, he was also a newspaper publisher and editor, publishing *The Quaker City*—which enhanced his reputation as a radical reformer against the elite—a weekly for some fifteen thousand readers.

A true romantic, he married his sweetheart, Rose Newman, twenty-six, on a large rock overlooking Wissahickon Creek. The couple had one child, but both Rose and the child died from tuberculosis in 1851, around the time that his sister Harriet and her two children died from the same disease. Suddenly, life's tragedies became too much for the fearless writer. He found it hard to go on. It is said that in his despondent state, he became suicidal and came very close to throwing himself off Niagara Falls but was talked out of it by friends.[12]

Lippard's role as a working-class hero did not preclude a talent for eloquent and powerful public speaking. When I read references to Lippard's talents as a speaker, I can only conclude that he spoke the King's English, meaning that he didn't fall prey to a world of grammatical and rhetorical blunders.

He contributed much to the mythology of the city, such as giving Philadelphia its sobriquet "the Quaker City." In his short story "Ring, Grandfather, Ring" (published in 1847), he details the doings of the Second Continental Congress at the signing of the Declaration of Independence and ends with a bit of fiction—how the signers of the Declaration rang the Liberty Bell atop Independence Hall so hard after the signing that the bell actually cracked.

Lippard's "how the Liberty Bell got its crack" story still manages to fool people. It is a testament to the power of his pen that fiction and myth have been allowed to override historical truth.

Lippard died at thirty-one years of age in 1854—of tuberculosis, just like his wife, sister and child before him. His death came well before the start of the Civil War, although it is said that his writings on slavery awakened Abraham Lincoln to the plight of slaves. Lippard's gothic, sensational style and his interest in esoteric spirituality give many of his works a prophetic ring. In his book *Monks of Monk Hall: A Romance of Philadelphia Life, Mystery, and Crime*, for instance, Lippard wrote that it was his intention to write a book that "describes all the phases of a corrupt social system, as manifested in the City of Philadelphia."

He continues:

> *To the young man or young woman who may read this book when I am dead, I have a word to say: Would to God that the evils recorded in these pages, were not based upon facts. Would to God that the experience of my life had not impressed me so vividly with the colossal vices and the terrible deformities, presented in the social system of this Large City, in the Nineteenth Century.*

EDGAR ALLAN POE, LIPPARD'S FRIEND, spent six of his most creative years in Philadelphia. The poet, short story writer, novelist and essayist lived at 532 North Seventh Street, and when he was not working as a magazine editor, he could be found floating on a barge on Fairmount Park's Wissachickon

Edgar Allan Poe. *Courtesy of the Library of Congress.*

Creek. Poe, in fact, was so fond of rafting on the Wissachickon that he often imaged the area "when the Demon of the Engine was not, when pic-nics were undreamed of and when the red man trod alone with the elk, upon the ridges that now lowered above."

Poe was born in Boston on January 19, 1809, to David and Elizabeth Poe, but by the time he was two years old, both his parents would be out of his life. His father would abandon the family to have children with other women, while his mother died, leaving Edgar in the care of his grandfather, who would arrange for him to be brought up by John and Frances Allan of Richmond, Virginia, both pious Scotch Presbyterians who saw fit to have him baptized on January 7, 1812, by Reverend John Buchanan.

The poet was later confirmed at Monumental Episcopal Church by Bishop Richard Channing. While this ceremony marked the end of his public

Edgar Allan Poe. *Courtesy of Jim Talone and the Philadelphia Mural Arts Program.*

religious affiliation, toward the end of his life he would spend considerable time with the Jesuits in New York.[13]

As a boy, Edgar was sent to school in England, where he showed unusual gifts as a poet. At seventeen, he enrolled in the University of Virginia, at the time an unorthodox school with a minimum of academic courses based on a design by the school's founder, Thomas Jefferson, who believed that students should be permitted to impose their own academic and recreational structure. Yet the university's free-form design proved detrimental to Poe's psyche: he left after one year, after finding himself deeply in debt.

After Poe's foster father, David, settled Edgar's debts, he was able to move back to Boston, where he worked on a newspaper until he decided to join the army, at which point he enlisted under the name Edgar Perry. He also listed his age as twenty-two although he was eighteen at the time. Once in the army, he was promptly shipped to South Carolina.

Soon after this, he would write and publish his first book of poetry, *Tamerlane and Other Poems*. A second volume would follow.

With his foster father's help, Poe was able to enroll as a cadet at West Point, although he left the school after a short while. He was probably the only West Point cadet who wrote satirical poems about the officers there.

At David Allan's death, Poe found himself disinherited. The reasons for the disinheritance were complex, some having to do with David Allan's involvements with other women, as well as his view of Poe's haphazard life of drinking, debt and the general misuse of money. Later in his life, Poe would speak kindly of Allan and say that his disinheritance was largely his own fault.

Life changed for the author of "The Raven," "The Tell-Tale Heart," "The Premature Burial" and "The Cask of Amontillado" when he took a wife, his thirteen-year-old cousin Virginia, although he was a seasoned twenty-six.

Poe traveled to Philadelphia with Virginia to work for magazines and found a position as editor with William E. Burton (*Burton's Magazine*), who paid him a small salary. As the years passed, Burton grew dissatisfied with Poe's work, although his main complaint was the poet's drinking, which often occurred at midday. After the relationship ended, Burton sold the magazine to George Graham, and Poe found himself as editor for the renamed publication, *Graham's Magazine*. Poe published many of his stories in these magazines, although "The Premature Burial" was published in 1844 in the *Philadelphia Dollar Newspaper*.

While in Philadelphia, he met George Lippard, forming a friendship that would last until his death. When Virginia died of tuberculosis in 1847, the

Edgar Allan Poe House. *Courtesy of Joe Nettis.*

poet's world would change once again. He published *Eureka, an Essay on the Material and Spiritual Universe,* that same year. In *Eureka,* Poe wrote:

> *Let us begin, then, at once, with that merest of words, "Infinity." This, like "God," "spirit," and some other expressions of which the equivalents exist in all languages, is by no means the expression of an idea—but of an effort at one. It stands for the possible attempt at an impossible conception. Man needed a term by which to point out the direction of this effort—the cloud*

behind which lay, forever invisible, the object of this attempt. A word, in fine, was demanded, by means of which one human being might put himself in relation at once with another human being and with a certain tendency of the human intellect. Out of this demand arose the word, "Infinity"; which is thus the representative but of the thought of a thought.

Poe moved to New York, where he became editor of the *Broadway Journal* and where he created some controversy when he accused Henry Wadsworth Longfellow of plagiarism. He was living in a cottage on the grounds of St. John's College (now Fordham University) and became friendly with the Jesuits when Virginia died. Virginia's death caused him great despair, although he took some comfort in his friendship with the Reverend Edward Doucet, SJ, who would allow him unlimited use of the college library. After Poe's death, Father Doucet recalled, "I knew him well. In bearing and countenance, he was extremely refined. His features were somewhat sharp and very thoughtful. He was well informed on all matters. I always thought he was a gentleman by nature and instinct."[14]

For his part, Poe thoroughly enjoyed the Jesuits and once said that they were "highly cultivated gentlemen and scholars, they smoked and they drank and they played cards, and they never said a word about religion."

Poe's "Hymn to the Virgin Mary" (1833) was published as part of "Morella" and was included as a "Catholic Hymn" in the 1845 edition of *"The Raven" and Other Poems*:

> *Sancta Maria! turn thine eyes*
> *Upon the sinner's sacrifice*
> *Of fervent prayer and humble love,*
> *From thy holy throne above.*

> *At morn, at noon, at twilight dim*
> *Maria! thou hast heard my hymn.*
> *In joy and wo, in good and ill*
> *Mother of God! be with us still.*

> *When my hours flew gently by,*
> *And no storms were in the sky,*
> *My soul, lest it should truant be—*
> *Thy love did guide to thine and thee.*

Now, when clouds of Fate o'ercast
All my Present, and my Past,
Let my Future radiant shine
With sweet hopes of thee and thine.[15]

On October 3, 1849, Poe was found in a delirious state on a street in Baltimore. He died several days later. At his funeral and burial in Westminster Cemetery in Baltimore's Presbyterian Church, only six to eight people were present. Some say that his last words were, "Lord, help my poor soul!" Although the diagnosis for his death was "mania a potu," or "madness from drinking," other causes cannot be ruled out, so the actual cause of death remains a mystery.

Before his death, he spent a couple of days in Philadelphia trying to find transportation money to Baltimore, and with a Philadelphia friend, John Sartain, who would later teach at the Pennsylvania Academy of the Fine Arts, he debated what to do while walking along the banks of the Schuylkill River.

Legend has it that Poe asked his friend Lippard for the transportation money. Since Lippard had just paid his rent, he couldn't help his friend, but he did help Poe raise the necessary funds.

A WRITER WHO DID NOT HAVE to have friends raise funds for him was Bayard Taylor, born in January 1825 in Kennett Square, Pennsylvania.

Taylor finished his schooling in 1842 and decided to become a painter. He apprenticed under Henry E. Evan in West Chester and wrote poetry in his spare time. He left Evans's tutelage for a trip to Europe in lieu of a university education. The publication of his first book of poems, *Ximena; or, the Battle of Sierra Morena, and Other Poems*, predated the publication of his travel essays in the *Saturday Evening Post*, whose offices were located on Philadelphia's Washington Square. He became engaged to his high school sweetheart, Mary S. Agnew, but the long engagement ended when she became sick with tuberculosis. The two were married for a mere two months before she died in December 1850.

With the publication of *Joseph and His Friend*, referred to by some as the first American gay novel, which was serialized in 1869 by the *Atlantic Monthly*, Taylor was called "the most outspoken advocate of 'the other love' in mid-century America.[16] At his death on December 19, 1878, he had published some fifty books and at least seven hundred newspaper and magazine articles.

Bayard Taylor. *Courtesy of Joseph A. Lordi and the Bayard Taylor Memorial Library.*

Pennsylvania writer Mark E. Dixon writes that after Mary Agnew was buried in December, eight months later, Taylor was off to Egypt:

> *Taylor was off again, this time to the Middle East. In Egypt, he met August Bufleb, a German businessman. Both men became enamored of the other. Bufleb wrote home to his wife that Taylor was "a glorious young man." "If it were not for you, I would go with him. He has won my love*

*by his amiability, his excellent heart, his pure spirit, in a degree of which I
did not believe myself capable."*

*Of Bufleb, Taylor told his mother, "When we speak of parting in a few
days, it brings the tears into our eyes."*[17]

Whatever was going on, Bufleb became an important friend. Taylor's
later visits at his home strengthened his interest in all things German. They
also introduced him to Marie Hansen (the niece of Bufleb's wife), whom
he would marry in 1857, and led to his appointment as U.S. ambassador in
Berlin. Taylor's confession to his mother in which he expresses his love for
Bufleb must be understood in the context of the time. An illustration that
comes to mind is the friendship between Joshua Fry Speed and the young
Abraham Lincoln, in which the young Lincoln enters Speed's Louisville store
and ends up asking him where he could find a room. Speed immediately
offers to share his own bed with Lincoln, which coincidentally happened to
be in a room above the store. The two men waste no time striking up a deal,
after which Lincoln returns to the store with his belongings. The two friends
would sleep in the same bed for four years.

Men in the 1800s often roomed or slept with other men in a single bed,
and little was thought of it. This was the Victorian era, when the art of male
friendship was in high bloom, when male friends would write long, intimate
letters to each other, often ending their letters with declarations of loyalty.
Living quarters (in the nineteenth century) were also tight. Whole families
lived and slept in one- or two-room houses, which means that they shared
every intimate part of their lives.

When Taylor was asked by the Centennial Commission in Philadelphia to
write a national hymn for the celebration, his competition was Walt Whitman.
Both poets submitted poems, but Whitman's poem was rejected.

Today, Whitman is considered America's greatest and most influential
poet. He lived just beyond Philadelphia in Camden, New Jersey, from 1873
until his death in 1892. Whitman revolutionized both the form and content
of poetry. His use of free verse established it as an accepted form of American
poetry. In the repressed atmosphere of the Victorian era, Whitman wrote
seriously about the body.

Whitman's career was a hodgepodge of newspaper editorships that
came and went. He was frequently getting into hot water or having
personality conflicts and editorial clashes with higher-ups. Then there
was his poetry—new, bold and way over the Victorian line. Bayard
Taylor, on the other hand, played the journalism game according to the

rules. He became respected, even beloved. When the 1876 centennial committee rejected Whitman's poem, the poet was hurt and even a little jealous that Taylor was accorded the honor.

Whitman's biographer, Jerome Loving, asks why the poet was surprised at the rejection. His poetry, after all, was causing some to call him "disgusting" and "vile"; even Taylor was calling the author of *Leaves of Grass* a "third-rate poet attempting to gratify his restless passion for personal notoriety." Taylor also condemned Whitman's repeated and unauthorized use of Ralph Waldo Emerson's letter as a preface in various editions of *Leaves of Grass*. Taylor was at the height of his fame when he was going around saying that Whitman's book was not fit to "be read aloud under the evening lamp."

Who knows what really motivated Taylor's attacks on the Camden poet. At the time, Taylor was a media darling, his fame worldwide. Whitman's impact, by contrast, lacked punch in the United States, although it was beginning to grow in Europe. Was all this merely jealous rivalry between two scribes? It seems so. To his credit, Taylor was no prude; he just knew how to play the polite society game. Even so, Taylor went so far as to dedicate *Joseph and His Friend* to those "who believe in the truth and tenderness of a man's love for man, as of man's love for woman: who recognize the trouble which confused ideas of life and the lack of high and intelligent culture bring upon a great portion of our country population. To all such, no explanation of this volume is necessary. Others will not read it."

But even Taylor was not immune to gossip in his Kennett Square neighborhood. He was not one to curtail his personal style because of these criticisms but thought of them as personal assaults, and he stood ready to defend himself at all times.

Growing up on Long Island, Walt Whitman's childhood was a lonely one. His father was convinced his son would be a failure and wanted to drive the poetry nonsense out of his head. As a young man, he worked as a legal assistant, printer, newspaper editor, writer and schoolteacher. These were the poet's salad years. At this time, he was fired from the *Brooklyn Daily Eagle* for writing a piece challenging the views of the paper's owner, Issac Van Anden. In his extreme youth, at twenty-one, he taught school. At that point, he was high strung and slender; some even say that he looked angry and troubled. In 1840, he wrote a letter to a friend about his experiences teaching school to the children of the farmers of Long Island. The letter gives no

Walt Whitman. *Courtesy of the New Jersey Division of Parks and Forestry, Walt Whitman House.*

indication that it was written by the poet who would one day come to be known as the poet of the masses:

> *I am sick of wearing away by inches, and spending the fairest portions of my little span of life. Here in this nest of bears, this forsaken of all God's creations, among clowns and country bumpkins, flat-heads, & coarse brown-faced girls, dirty, ill-formed young brats, with squalling throats & crude manners, & bog-trotters, with all the disgusting conceit*

of ignorance & vulgarity. It is enough to make the fountains of good-will dry up in our hearts.[18]

In Southold, Long Island, where Whitman taught school, he stayed at the home of George Wells, living with Wells and his wife and several children. Teachers or professors then were often considered members of the family and slept with the children they taught.

Reverend Ralph Smith, a Presbyterian minister, accused Whitman from the pulpit of being a sodomite and, in connection with that, mentioned the name of the boy and the family's name where he was staying. Something happened in that house, but what? Or did it? The record is not clear. Although records were kept of Reverend Smith's sermons, the twelve or so pages that refer to Whitman's situation were mysteriously eliminated from the Smith archive, at least according to reports by people who claimed to have seen them.

This much is known: After Reverend Smith's sermon, all hell broke loose. A mob, hot tar buckets in hand, went to the home of George Wells expecting to find Whitman. The poet was not there, however. He was hiding in one of the bedrooms, perhaps under a bed or in the attic at the local doctor's house. The mob found him and dragged him outside, where they painted his hair and clothing with tar and then led him to a wagon with the intention of driving him out of town. Yet before things got really violent, a woman saved him. She yelled at the mob and told them to leave him alone, so everyone dispersed like grammar school children at the conclusion of recess.

It took the poet a good month to recover from his wounds, both physical and psychological, although quite sensibly he opted to leave Southold at that time. His sister Mary continued to stay there, and the poet would return periodically for short visits.[19]

Whitman lovers know what Abraham Lincoln meant to the bard, namely by elegies such as "When Lilacs Last in the Dooryard Bloom'd" and the schoolboy poem "O Captain! My Captain!" Biographies of Whitman inevitably refer to the poet's fascination with, and love for, Abraham Lincoln, despite the fact that historians and students of history know that there was no real friendship between the two men. In fact, the closest they came to meeting was one Halloween night when Whitman happened to be in the White House to pick up a set of round-trip train tickets to New York so he could go home and vote in the 1863 elections. Lincoln's secretary, John Hay, handed Whitman the tickets as the poet caught a glimpse of Lincoln talking with a friend in an adjoining room. "His face & manner have an expression…inexpressibly sweet—one hand on his friend's shoulder the other holding his hand," Whitman wrote of that moment.[20]

Most biographers agree that Whitman and Lincoln had frequent distant eye-to-eye contact in Washington. Lincoln, in fact, had read Whitman's *Leaves of Grass* in his Springfield law office in 1857. Lincoln's law clerk at the time, Billy Herndon, a rabid collector of books, had bought a copy of *Leaves of Grass* after reading that Ralph Waldo Emerson called it "the most extraordinary piece of wit and wisdom that America has yet contributed." Herndon shared his copy with the future president. Later, Lincoln, with his long legs resting on the edge of his desk, couldn't put *Leaves of Grass* down, but when he brought the book home, it barely managed to escape being burned.

No doubt, Lincoln read the following lines from *Leaves of Grass*:

> *I bequeath myself to the dirt to grow from the grass I love,*
> *If you want me again look for me under your bootsoles.*

> *You will hardly know who I am or what I mean,*
> *But I shall be good health to you nevertheless,*
> *And filter and fibre your blood.*
> *Failing to fetch me at first keep encouraged,*
> *Missing me one place search another,*
> *I stop somewhere waiting for you.*

Despite his family's fiery disapproval of Whitman, Lincoln was a truth seeker and not about to dismiss the poet's work as vulgar. After all, Lincoln was so homespun that he once caused Herndon to remark that the young lawyer "never could see the harm in wearing a sack-coat instead of a swallowtail to an evening party, nor could he realize the offense of telling a vulgar yarn if a preacher happened to be present."

Like Lincoln, Whitman was a man very much out of touch when it came to clothing himself or mingling with Washington society. With his ragged clothes and Wild Buffalo Bill hats and jackets, no wonder he had doubts about many of the politicians he had met, especially the fastidious Boston abolitionist Charles Sumner, who lived on Hancock Street in Beacon Hill and who was so in love with his own hands that he would study them as they rested on his crossed legs.

In the late 1980s, an elderly tour guide at the Walt Whitman House in Camden was fond of telling visitors that "Mr. Whitman was not a homosexual!" She would mention that Whitman's nurse, Mary Oakes Davis, had been in love with him. Then she was fond of quoting Whitman's infamous line to John Addington Symonds when Symonds confronted the poet on the homoerotic content of the Calamus poems in *Leaves of Grass*: "I am fain to hope that the pages themselves are not to be even mentioned for such gratuitous and quite at the time undreamed and unwished possibility of morbid influences—which are disavowed by me and seem damnable."

On the surface, these words seem pretty clear—even if Edward Carpenter, a contemporary of Symonds, knew that Whitman was telling a lie. Carpenter blamed Whitman's cowardice on the social atmosphere of 1891. Carpenter actually came out and said that he slept with Whitman, and he gave details of the encounter to a writer named Arthur Gavin. As for the poet's off-putting letter to Symonds, Charley Shively, in *Calamus Lovers: Walt Whitman's Working Class Camerados*, states that "Whitman wasn't ready to join Symonds in a crusade for gay rights," although he was quick to praise Symonds's poem "Love and Death," which honored two Athenian male lovers "who sacrificed themselves in the war against Sparta."[21]

"Comrade love," Shively writes, "was thus presented as less selfish than family love, which was concerned with procreation more than community...Whitman's problem with Symonds was that the Englishman wasn't enough of a democrat."

Whitman had special male friends like ex-Confederate soldier Peter Doyle (a thin Irishman who was the poet's primary companion in Camden for fifteen years), Warren Fritzenger (the male nurse who took Whitman along the Camden waterfront in his wheelchair), William Sydnor (a guy who drove a Pittsburgh streetcar), David Fender ("a redhaired young man," Whitman wrote), John Ferguson ("tall and slender") and Willy Hayes ("a drummer in a marine band"). There was also Walter Dean, whom Whitman met in Philadelphia's John Wanamaker's department store (John Wanamaker, the so-called King of Merchants, banned *Leaves of Grass* from Wanamaker's bookstore). And there were more. The Whitman House guide had no comments on Oscar Wilde's famous remark when Wilde was asked by George Ives in London whether the American poet was "one of the Greek Lovers." Ives asked the big question after Wilde's visit to the poet's brother's house at 431 Stevens Street in Camden (now demolished), where Whitman lived from 1873 to 1884.

Wilde at that time told Ives, "Of course, I have the kiss of Walt Whitman still on my lips," but he didn't say any more. The "of course" speaks volumes. Literary history is full of stories about how Whitman dealt with women who wrote him love letters, including unflattering and shocking descriptions of Mary Davies (the woman praised by the tour guide) as one who preyed on widowers for their inheritances.

"LITERATURE, OF ALL THE ARTS," Muriel Spark once wrote, "is the most penetrable into the human life of the world, for the simple reason that words are our common currency. We don't instinctively, from morning to night, paint pictures to each other, or play music to each other, in order to communicate; we talk, we write to each other."[22]

So it was with Owen Wister, the only child of a physician father and an actress mother who happened to be the daughter of English actress Fanny Kemble. The Wister family had strong Philadelphia patrician roots; as an only child, young Wister was sent to exclusive boarding schools in New England and Switzerland.

From this tableau of breeding, in 1878 Wister entered Harvard, where he achieved top honors in musical composition and dramatic writing. Perhaps it was his success in writing the libretto for Hasty Pudding's comic opera *Dido and Aeneas* that made him want to become a composer.

Despite his mother's artistic leanings (she was a magazine writer), Wister's father was not keen on his son's ambition to study musical composition in Paris. The prospect, no doubt, appeared naïve to the grounded family physician, but in the end he gave his consent and even provided the young student with financial support.

Now there was nothing standing in the way of Owen's becoming a great composer. He had only to build from scratch and start a legacy as great as Chopin's—provided, of course, that he could turn his dream into reality. For most artists, such an achievement is rarely a straight, unencumbered road but a crooked one filled with unexpected pitfalls.

But Wister's Parisian musical ambitions must have hit rock bottom because in 1883 he opted to return to the Quaker City after resigning himself to a utilitarian goal: a junior position in a Philadelphia law firm, something that for many young men would have been a fine thing, indeed, although in Wister's case it led to dissatisfaction and restlessness.

He tried his hand at another artistic endeavor, coauthoring a novel with a Harvard friend, before entering Harvard Law School. Yet as the enrollment date for law school drew near, Wister was on the verge of a collapse. Psychoanalytical experts term this a nervous breakdown—complete, of course, with a breakdown's unattractive antecedents like vertigo, blinding headaches and hallucinations.

His father urged him to leave Paris at once, and the much-weakened Wister complied, although he had now developed Bell's palsy and would have to wait a few weeks for its eventual remission.[23]

Nervous breakdowns, when they happen to artists, can sometimes be a ticket to literary and intellectual insight. The number of poets and

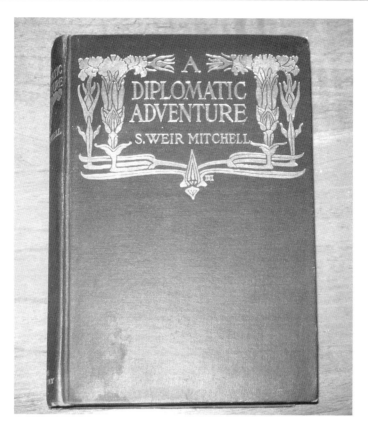

S. Weir Mitchell's *A Diplomatic Adventure. Courtesy of Greg Gillespie.*

novelists who have sought refuge in sanatoriums or in warmer climates after a breakdown are legion.

In Philadelphia, Wister consulted Dr. S. Weir Mitchell, a Franklin Inn member and also a friend of essayist Agnes Repplier. Wister was diagnosed with a severe case of neurasthenia and suggested a trip to a Wyoming ranch. Mitchell had developed a system for treating nervous men, and that was to send them to the West, where they could rope cattle, hunt game, rough ride horses and engage in various forms of male bonding.[24] In his 1871 book, *Wear and Tear*, Mitchell encouraged nervous men to go west in order to reinforce their masculinity and to test their willpower. "Under great nervous stress," Mitchell wrote, "the strong man becomes like the average woman."[25]

Had Wister been born today, his attending physician no doubt would never have suggested that he travel west for his health, as was the custom of the day, but instead be put on a regime of psychotropic meds that

Thomas Eakins House. *Courtesy of Mural Arts of Philadelphia.*

could have deadened both his energy and creative talents—"like a patient etherized upon a table."

The "go west" cure for men was a staple of nineteenth-century life. For Philadelphia artist Thomas Eakins, who was fired from the Pennsylvania Academy of the Arts for removing the loincloth of a male model in front of female students and who was then ostracized by Philadelphia society, going west was more than rehabilitative. It saved his life.

"For some days I have been quite cast down being cut deliberately on the street by those who have every occasion to know me," Eakins wrote in a letter to his sister.

Eakins sought his western cure in the Dakotas, and when he returned, he was "built up miraculously," according to Walt Whitman.

Whitman himself sought his own western cure in 1879 and documented that journey in *Specimen Days* (1882).

Even Rough Rider Teddy Roosevelt returned from his western cure without what his detractors called his "former effeminate looks" and "high voice that often provided comparison to Oscar Wilde."[26]

After three weeks in Wyoming, Wister—who had slept in a tent, bathed in an icy creek, hunted, fished and spent hours on horseback—felt like a new man.

Dr. Mitchell also prescribed "rest cures" for women. Charlotte Perkins Gilman, who wrote about Mitchell in *The Yellow Wallpaper* (1892), was once a patient of his, but the treatment was quite different. Instead of open skies, campfires at night and swims in the local creek, for nervous women, Mitchell advocated seclusion, overfeeding, electrotherapy and massage.[27]

Although competent historians have come to categorize Mitchell's rest cure therapy for women as nothing more than nineteenth-century misogyny, Wister was so entranced by the beauty he experienced in Wyoming that he came to idolize the cowboy, which in turn would form the basis for his classic novel *The Virginian: A Horseman of the Plains*, about a Wyoming cattleman who would go on to become one of the country's first mass-market bestsellers.

"To Wister," Kimmel writes, "the west was 'manly, egalitarian, self reliant, and Aryan'—it was the true America, far from the feminizing, immigrant infected cities, where voracious blacks and masculine women devoured white men's chances to demonstrate manhood."[28]

Wister would spend the next fifteen years traveling to Wyoming during the summer months, visiting ranches, cow camps and remote cavalry outposts while getting to know gamblers and ranch hands. These sojourns provided him with stories that he began publishing in *Harper's Weekly*. The publication of *The Virginian* in 1902 changed his life forever. The book sold 200,000 copies in one year and was adapted for Broadway; it went on to be the basis for five movies and a television series.

The Virginian has never been out of print, despite the story's stock character stereotypes, namely the eastern "naïve" narrator, the savage Indian, the puritanical schoolmarm and the devil-may-care, tobacco-chewing cattle rustler.

In Chapter 4 of *The Virginian*, Wister writes:

> *Morning had been for some while astir in Medicine Bow before I left my quilts. The new day and its doings began around me in the store, chiefly at the grocery counter. Dry-goods were not in great request. The early rising cow-boys were off again to their work; and those to whom their night's holiday had left any dollars were spending these for tobacco, or cartridges, or canned provisions for the journey to their distant camps. Sardines were called for, and potted chicken, and devilled ham: a sophisticated nourishment, at first sight, for these sons of the sage-brush. But portable ready-made food plays of necessity a great part in the opening of a new country. These*

picnic pots and cans were the first of her trophies that Civilization dropped upon Wyoming's virgin soil. The cow-boy is now gone to worlds invisible; the wind has blown away the white ashes of his camp-fires; but the empty sardine box lies rusting over the face of the Western earth.

The book caused Wister to become more famous than his friend novelist Henry James, whom Wister revered and thought of as "a real novelist." In a curious twist of fate, the recognition that he sought for his musical compositions in Paris was now his but in triplicate, yet this made him decidedly unhappy because he looked on his fans as "the semi-literate public." He wanted Henry James's fan base, not "the repugnant masses."

After writing and publishing *The Virginian*, Wister returned to Philadelphia after realizing that his western ideal wasn't what it used to be. He complained of "the rabble of excessive democracy, populist politicians, unassimilated immigrants and tourists." In Philadelphia, he dabbled in many things, especially politics and writing nonfiction, including the story of his friendship with Teddy Roosevelt, *Roosevelt: The Story of a Friendship*.

Wister died on July 21, 1938, in Rhode Island. His journals and letters, edited by Frances Kimble Wister, were published in 1958.

NOT MANY WRITERS CAN CLAIM to be a spiritual descendent of the infamous occultist Aleister Crowley, but one Philadelphia writer holds that title.

Charles Godfrey Leland was born on August 15, 1824, to merchant Charles Leland and Charlotte Godfrey, both direct descendents of the first settlers of New England. Young Charles's boyhood was a mixture of privileged wealth and an obsession with the mystical. He loved folk magic and walking in the woods, where he claimed that he heard words in the songs of birds and even in the sound of running water. At eighteen years of age, he wrote his first book, *Hermes Trismegistus: His Divine Pymander*. The book was later published and became an inspiration for a variety of hermetic writings.

Charles graduated from the College of New Jersey, now Princeton University, in 1845. After graduation, he studied in Munich, Germany, and then traveled in Europe. In his book *Memoirs*, he writes about the physical impression he made as a young man: "At this time I was a trifle over six feet two in height, and had then and for some time after so fair a red and white complexion, that the young ladies in Philadelphia four years later teased me by spreading the report that I used rouge and white paint! I was not as yet 'filled out,' but held myself straightly, and was fairly proportioned."

After his postgraduate European travels, he returned to Philadelphia to begin a career in journalism, during which he wrote for, and edited, a number of newspapers and magazines, including the *Philadelphia Evening Bulletin*, the *Philadelphia Press* and *Vanity Fair*. During the Civil War, he enlisted in the Union army, but his experiences on the battlefield were limited.

In 1870, he moved to England, where his mystic inclinations and fluency in several languages helped him immerse himself in gypsy society, studying their culture to such an extent that in time he came to be accepted as one of their own. In Florence, he met Maddalena, a famous Tarot card reader in the back streets of the city. This association led to his discovery of a number of witch cults with roots going back to ancient times.[29]

In his book *Arcadia, or the Gospel of the Witches*, Leland wrote:

> *So long ago as the year 1886 I learned that there was in existence a manuscript setting forth the doctrines of Italian witchcraft, and I was promised that, if possible, it should be obtained for me. In this I was for a time disappointed. But having urged it on Maddalena, my collector of folk-lore, while she was leading a wandering life in Tuscany, to make an effort to obtain or recover something of the kind, I at last received from her, on January 1, 1897, entitled* Arcadia, or the Gospel of the Witches.

Leland had been well schooled from childhood in the world of spirits. In *Memoirs*, for instance, he writes about the haunted feeling many felt in Philadelphia's Washington Square:

> *Washington Square, opposite our house, had been in the olden time a Potter's Field, where all the victims of the yellow fever pestilence had been interred. Now it had become a beautiful little park, but there were legends of a myriad of white confused forms seen flitting over it in the night, for it was a mysterious haunted place to many still, and I can remember my mother gently reproving one of our pretty neighbours for repeating such tales.*[30]

Leland's rich exploration of European witchcraft in books such as *The English Gypsies and Their Language* (1873), *Egyptian Sketch Book* (1873), *The Minor Arts* (1880), *The Gypsies* (1882), *Gypsy Sorcery and Fortune Telling* (1891) and *Legends of Florence* (1895–96) enabled him to look at Philadelphia through a metaphysical lens. In *Memoirs*, he writes about witches in the Quaker City:

As for the black witch, as there were still four negro sorcerers in Philadelphia in 1883 (I have their addresses), it may be imagined to what an extent Voodoo still prevailed among our Ebony men and brothers. Of one of there my mother had a sad experience. We had a black cook named Ann Lloyd, of whom, to express it mildly, one must say that she was "no good." My mother dismissed her, but several who succeeded her left abruptly. Then it was found that Ann, who professed, had put a spell of death on all who should take her place. My mother learned this, and when the last black cook gave warning she received a good admonition as to a Christian being a slave to the evil one. I believe that this ended the enchantment.[31]

Leland's works also include *The Breitmann Ballads* (1895), which made him famous as a poet, and *Life of Abraham Lincoln* (1879), in which he recounts Lincoln's strength as a young man. Leland recounts how, while working as a ferryman to manage a boat that crossed the Ohio River and Anderson Creek, Lincoln also worked as a hostler, ground corn and built fires. "Though he was obliged to rise so early," he wrote,

he always studied till nearly midnight. He was in great demand when hogs were slaughtered. For this rough work he was paid 31 cents a day. Meanwhile, he became incredibly strong. He could carry six hundred pounds with ease; he once picked up some huge posts which four men were about to lift, and bore them away with little effort. Men yet alive have seen him lift a full barrel of liquor and drink from the bung-hole…He was especially skilled in wrestling, and from the year 1828 there was no man, far or near, who would compete with him in it.[32]

As the founder and first director of the Public Industrial Art School of Philadelphia, now known as University of the Arts, Leland attracted the admiration of Oscar Wilde. While lecturing to an audience in Montreal, Wilde praised the philosophy of arts education Leland had developed and stated, "I would have a workshop attached to every school…I have seen only one such school in the United States, and was founded by my friend Leland. I stopped there yesterday, and have brought some of their work to show you."

Before his death in Florence on March 20, 1903, Philadelphia's own Aleister Crowley, who published almost two dozen books in his lifetime, wrote of his impressions of the city after a long sojourn in Europe:

Its inhabitants were all well-bathed, well-clad, well-behaved; all with exactly the same ideas and the same ideals. A decided degree of refinement was everywhere perceptible, and they were so fond of flowers that I once ascertained by careful inquiry that in most respectable families there was annually much more money expended for bouquets than for books.[33]

AT THE OPPOSITE END OF NEO-PAGANISM is a nearly forgotten Catholic writer who, during the course of her literary career, introduced Philadelphia audiences to novelist Henry James, was lauded by Edith Wharton and even shared a drink with poet Walt Whitman. She was a woman who took care of her disabled brother, Louis, walking miles each week to care for him in his apartment in another part of the city.

Born in 1855, Agnes Repplier went to the Convent of the Sacred Heart, Eden Hall, in Philadelphia's Torresdale section. She was a headstrong, independent, mischievous girl. Her mischief making resulted in expulsion from Eden Hall, although her mother later enrolled her in the Agnes Irwin School, where she was again expelled, this time for showing her refusal to read a required book by throwing it on the floor. It didn't help her student reputation any that she began smoking Benson & Hedges cigarettes when she was eleven years old, a brand she would continue to smoke until her death in 1950 at age ninety-five. (Reflecting on her days at Eden Hall, Repplier remarked that her only big accomplishment there was learning to smoke and that she was able to obtain the cigarettes from one of the girls' brothers, who smuggled them in for her.)

In her first book, *In Our Convent Days* (1905), Repplier recounts what her days were like in Eden Hall, especially after daily morning Mass, when the students were allowed to speak only in French to their classmates at the breakfast table:

At that Spartan meal…even had we been able or willing to employ the hated medium [French], there was practically no one to talk to. By a triumph of monastic discipline, we were placed at table, and at church, next to girls whom we had nothing to say; good girls, with medals around their necks, and blue or green ribbons over their shoulders, who served as insulating mediums, as non-conductors, separating us from cheerful currents of speech.

The little girl who would grow up to be called "a shy Catholic version of Ralph Waldo Emerson" and "the American Jane Austen" did not have an easy

Agnes Repplier. *Courtesy of Vintage Photographs.*

beginning, but her rebellious streak may have had familial roots. Mrs. Repplier was a committed Southerner with a loyalty to the Confederate South, while Mr. Repplier was a staunch Unionist. Mr. Repplier, in fact, was unhappy with his wife's aiding the Confederate cause by sending regular boxes of food and wine to Southern prisoners at nearby Fort Delaware. When General Lee surrendered to Union forces on April 15, 1865, the Repplier family joined thousands of Philadelphians in the celebration. The wild cacophony of bonfires, ringing church bells and impromptu parades happening all over town changed a few days later with Abraham Lincoln's assassination. As the body of the former president made its way through the center of town, the procession passed the corner of Twenty-first and Chestnut Street, where young Agnes stood with her family and watched as the catafalque was drawn by several horses.

George Stewart Stokes, in his 1949 biography, *Agnes Repplier, Lady of Letters*, describes the scene at Twenty-first and Chestnut:

> *Suddenly a voice rose in frantic shouting, piercing the doleful music. The onlookers turned in horror to see a young girl, enchanted by the spectacle, jumping up and down, clapping her hands in ecstatic glee. Mr. Repplier was furious. It was one of the maids from his household making the disgraceful demonstration.*

Mr. Repplier, afraid that the crowd would be moved to anger or even violence, frantically ushered the maid down a side street.

Agnes's expulsion from school exposed her to what she called "stupid, monotonous, everlasting home duties,"[34] despite the fact that, at age sixteen, she was already embarking on a course of self-education. She perfected her French and Latin, read and reread Horace and then tried her hand at becoming a writer by submitting stories, small articles and poems to various Philadelphia newspapers. Eventually, she achieved some success when she submitted pieces to the *Catholic World* and then, after many attempts, to the *Atlantic Monthly*. At this time, she was living apart from her family at 4015 Locust Street and traveling daily into town in order to work in the libraries there. Although Agnes had every opportunity to do research at the University of Pennsylvania Library, she felt uncomfortable in that setting and preferred the more familiar stacks at the Library Company, especially at the Ridgeway Branch on South Broad Street, although she found the building to be a misbegotten place, "dark, dismal, depressing, inconvenient…a haunting horror."[35]

The *Catholic World*, where many of Repplier's early essays appeared, was founded by Father Isaac Thomas Hecker, a Catholic convert who had once lived among the New England Transcendentalists and who had been close friends with both Ralph Waldo Emerson (his teacher) and Henry David Thoreau (whom he made a serious effort to convert after his own conversion). Father Hecker was a mystic, writer and theologian who founded the Missionary Priests of St. Paul the Apostle (the Paulist Order) in 1865 and the *Catholic World* in 1872. Repplier met him in person for the first time in 1884, when she was twenty-nine years old, during a trip to New York City, ostensibly to visit the offices of the magazine. At that time, she had already published one story in the *Catholic World*, "A Story of Nuremberg," but as Stokes states, Father Hecker "had had his full of Repplierean romance" and suggested to Repplier that she forget fiction and stick to the essay form.

Home of Agnes Repplier. *Author's collection.*

Repplier wrote of that meeting some twenty-five years later: "Father Hecker told me that my stories were mechanical, and gave no indication of being transcripts from life. 'I fancy,' he said, 'that you know more about books than you do about life, that you are more a reader than an observer.'"

Immediately after Father Hecker's suggestion, Repplier wrote an essay on Ruskin that, she said, "turned my feet into the path which I have trodden laboriously ever since." "Ruskin as a Teacher" considers the English critic's anti-Catholic attitude and then laments that he didn't go further in order to discover the "holiness of Catholic art." Repplier felt that in his early works, Ruskin was already on an evolutionary path toward Catholicism but that this path had been impeded. She ends her essay in neutral high gear by agreeing with Ruskin "that work done for commercial gain does not succeed."[36]

Later, in a response to an article entitled "The Young Catholic Writer: What Shall He Do?" in which a Protestant minister argues that the novice Catholic writer should "conceal his faith…lest it blight his literary reputation," Repplier replies, "When faith is the most vital thing in life, when it is the source of our wildest sympathies and of the deepest feelings, when we owe to it whatever distinction of mind and harmony of soul we possess, we cannot push it intentionally out of sight without growing flat and dry through insincerity." She then explains that the one book she wrote for "her own people" (*In Our Convent Days*), "has been read with perfect good humor by a secular public." She goes on to say, "It is impossible for me to believe that anybody cares what catechism I studied when I was a child, or what Church I go to now."[37]

By 1885, the Eden Hall/Agnes Irwin School dropout was living the life of a writer.

From Stokes we learn that

> *every morning, promptly at nine, Miss Repplier would proceed to her study and take her place at a tidy desk watched over by a portrait of Keats after Severn's sketch. Though she had heard and read that some authors wrote their best at night because of the thought-conducive quiet, Agnes Repplier found that for her the morning was the most propitious time of all.*

Agnes was glad to take her first trip to Europe after the death of her parents, a sojourn that included a trip to Berlin, where she noted that the public discipline evident on the streets was so strict that she feared arrest for some minor infraction. She discovered that she preferred London to Paris, though she found much to admire in Rome, especially the graves of Shelley and Keats and, of course, the Catacombs, where she wrote to a friend, Harrison Morris, how she listened to a Trappist monk guide who had been released from his vows of silence for the occasion and whom, she quipped, "certainly made up for lost time."

Back in Philadelphia, she was always pleased when she could find an apartment within walking distance to the Church of Saint John Evangelist, once the city's cathedral before the construction of Saints Peter and Paul on the Benjamin Franklin Parkway. In Philadelphia, much of Repplier's social life consisted of visiting and speaking at many of the city's small literary and conversation clubs. Philadelphia, especially in Repplier's time, was often referred to as the city of clubs.

At the southeast corner of Broad and Locust Streets, for instance, stood the remains of the Hotel Walton (later renamed the John Bartram Hotel), a dark, Draconian-looking palace designed by Angus "Anxious" Wade, an artist who later became an architect. Opened in 1896, the ornate interior included Pompeian brick, vaulted ceilings, symmetrical stairs and Elizabethan strapped pattern ceilings. The hotel was demolished in 1966, but in Repplier's time it was a regal place.

There was Camac Street, or "the Little Street of Clubs," with its fine array of two-story nineteenth-century structures that housed some of the most artistic and Bohemian clubs in the city. Often referred to as Egg Head Row, on this one-block radius between Walnut Street and Locust, one can find the Sketch Club, the nation's oldest artists' club; the Plastic Club, the nation's oldest arts club for women; and the Franklin Inn Club, founded in 1902.

The Franklin Inn Club was originally founded as a meeting place for literary artists and journalists. In Repplier's time, it was for men only, so she was never a member, although she spoke at the Contemporary Club, founded in 1886. Contemporary Club luncheons were devoted to the exchange of ideas and to the hot topics of the day. Guest speakers included Margaret Singer and poet Walt Whitman. Repplier, in fact, spoke there often, except when she was asked to participate in a debate on Shakespeare and had to decline, saying, "I do not assign to myself the task of imparting what I don't know to the world."[38] Contemporary Club members valued Repplier for her ad hoc statements when the talks were turned over to the audience. Referred to as "Agnes Reply-er" during these occasions, she would often debate with journalist Talcott ("Talk-Talk") Williams of the *Philadelphia Press*.

In 1886, Repplier was able to get Walt Whitman to address the Contemporary Club, although when the big day came, her misgivings about the poet's country farmer clothes magnified significantly when she pondered what kind of speech he was getting ready to deliver. Her fears were alleviated when the poet did not disappoint but spoke "beautifully, well within bounds, and with a charming and grave manner." Sometime later, she introduced novelist Henry James to Contemporary Club members, but the impeccably groomed author of *Portrait of a Lady*, *Washington Square* and *The Ambassadors* proved to be a major disappointment to most of the members. Only Repplier's hearty introduction was the high point of the day.

Repplier wrote several biographies, most of which have Catholic themes, including *Mere Marie of the Ursulines*, *Pere Marquette* and *Junipero Serra: Pioneer Colonist of California*. Referring to early Native Americans in *Pere Marquette*, she wrote that "fear, the blind unreasoning fear of superstition, rules the savage heart" and then went on to describe how the missionaries were viewed by the "savages":

> *An Indian woman would watch a priest like a hawk, lest he should baptize her dying infant. Those drops of water, she believed, would hasten death. The sign of the cross was dreaded as invoking peril. The grave abstracted manner in which the missionaries read their breviaries awakened lively apprehension. Why should the strangers fix their profound attention upon those little black books unless they were pronouncing incantations?*

In *Junipero Serra*, Repplier tells the story of how Serra guided the Franciscans in the establishment of missions in northern California after the Jesuits were driven out of the territory. Her story focuses on the clash of native populations with the "morality" of the western missionaries. In one passage, she relates how the young novelist Richard Dana (*Two Years Before the Mast*) was "well fed at the missions" but "badly fed elsewhere." Why the missions eventually failed in later years, Repplier explains, can be traced to an existence that was "perpetually threatened":

> *From the time that the Mexican republic was established, it never ceased its efforts at secularization. Two things only stood in its way: the amazing but none the less undeniable reluctance of the Indians to be emancipated, and the oft-repeated fact that seven eighths of the country's produce was raised in the missions. Their dissolution would mean the collapse of industry and trade.*

Describing herself as a devout Catholic, Repplier nevertheless detested a hagiologist tendency in Catholic literature when it came to the lives of the saints. In her essay "Goodness and Gaiety," she writes that the saints of heaven "shine dimly through a nebulous haze of hagiology." She decries these "embodiments of inaccessible virtues, as remote from us and from our neighbors as if they lived on another planet." She lauds Cardinal Newman, "who first entered a protest against 'minced saints,' [and] against the pious and popular custom of chopping up human records into lessons for the devout."

About hagiologists, she said, "In their desire to be edifying, they cease to be convincing."

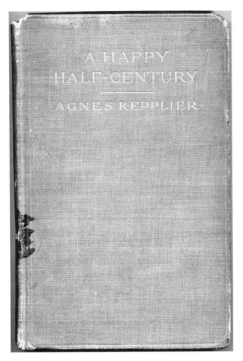

Courtesy of Greg Gillespie.

Although she describes her first Holy Week in Rome as "scrubby little affairs," when she knelt at the feet of Pope Leo XIII in 1903, something happened during that meeting. "I knelt at his feet for fully ten minutes, and he held my hand all the time, save when he laid his own hands on my head to bless me."

Emma Repplier, the writer's niece, wrote in a 1957 memoir of her aunt that during a visit to Constantinople, Agnes visited the Mosque of Saint Sofia and found it "surpassingly beautiful, even in its degradation." The tone changes to that of a prophetess when Emma reports that her aunt predicted "that the church will one day be restored to Christian hands forever" because "over the Apse rests the figure of Our Lord, concealed yet dimly visible, a sign and a token that the hour of reparation will come."[39]

By 1900, Philadelphia's own "Jane Austen" had already won the admiration and respect of the biggest names in literature, among them Edith Wharton, poet Walt Whitman and novelist Henry James. Among her friends she counted artist Cecilia Beaux, novelist Owen Wister and poet Amy Lowell.

"There isn't a writer in the country who hasn't been trying to achieve the perfection of style of the distinguished Miss Repplier," Edith Wharton said after their 1906 meeting in Lenox, Massachusetts.

When Repplier visited the poet Walt Whitman, Stokes writes that "she found him a most astounding old man, though very simple, kind, and hospitable."

The fact that Whitman was boarding in Camden when they met was, for Repplier, a most depressing reality. She felt that being a boarder was one of the most depressing ways anybody could live and added that the reason the great poet had such difficulty in getting along in life could be traced to his living in a city like Camden.

During that first meeting, the poet did his gracious best: he served her whiskey in a china toothbrush mug, having no shot glasses on hand. Stokes writes that Agnes drank the drink "heroically" and then goes on to quote her thoughts about the condition of Whitman's rooms: "His little room was littered with old newspapers, so that one lighted match carelessly discarded would send him into another world."

She also felt that while Whitman wrote a few great lines of poetry worth remembering, most of it was not worth remembering. Stokes concludes:

> *She recognized that he* [Whitman] *always had the courage to be just what he wanted to be, that he never allowed anything to interfere with his life, and this she found an admirable quality. But she felt him to be an incurable poseur. He loved his indecency, she insisted, clinging to it with almost embarrassing ardor.*

During her lifetime, Repplier turned down artist Thomas Eakins when he approached her about painting her portrait. She was afraid of Eakins's emphasis on realism. In explaining her refusal, she said that as a tall, thin woman, she'd probably have an easier time with Eakins than she would if she had been born "dumpy."

The 1844-born Thomas Eakins went to Central High School, where he learned technical drawing. In 1886, he went to Paris, catching French realism before it evolved into Impressionism. From Paris, he wrote to his father that a real artist does not sit down monkey-like and copy a coalscuttle or an ugly woman verbatim like a Dutch painter but that he's careful to keep a sharp eye on Nature. In Paris, he learned to have no shame about bodies or sex, a fact that would cause him trouble on his return to the Quaker City. The year 1870 found him in his parents' house on Mount Vernon Street, where he'd set up a portrait studio, doing pictures and portraits of society people and members of the Roman Catholic hierarchy. His sporting pictures include such masterpieces as *Max Schmitt in a Single Scull* and *Pushing for the Rail*. He exhibited at a Philadelphia gallery in 1896, an event that was ignored by the local press. When the Pennsylvania Academy awarded him the Temple Gold Medal for a portrait of an archbishop, Eakins accepted it wearing red bicycle pants and then gave the medal to the U.S. Mint, where it was melted down. He died on June 25, 1916. He was buried in a forgotten West Philadelphia plot that remained unmarked until 1983.

Turning down Eakins probably contributed to Repplier's feeling that she was underappreciated in her hometown. In her book *Philadelphia: The Place and the*

People, she wrote that the Quaker City lacked discriminating enthusiasm for her own children…which enabled more zealous towns to rend the skies with shrill paeans of applause." She added, "If mistaking geese for swans produces sad confusion…the mistaking of swans for geese may also be a serious error. The birds either languish or fly away to keener air." What Repplier had in mind were those Philadelphians who left the city for more welcoming environments.

Repplier's writing career lasted sixty-five years, yet in order to experience the fullness of her reading public's appreciation, she had to travel to Boston. Stokes has this to say about Repplier's treatment in her hometown:

> *If her head had been understandably turned by Boston, it was swiftly unturned again by Philadelphia. Back home, she was merely Agnes Repplier, a relatively insignificant writer living quietly west of the Schuylkill. Here she found no open-arms reception and this in spite of her "triumph" in Boston. Here she found only obscurity, the obscurity, she felt, that is Philadelphia itself.*

While the essayist never married, she found solace in her cats, especially Agrippina. "Cats like quiet people. They heartily approve of a sedentary life. Cats are without morals," she wrote,

> *and they are perfectly democratic. Dogs are snobs, preferring a mate of their own class. But as for cats, any old tom in the alley will please them. Consider Agrippina. She had a black lover, an alley lover. But he suited her. She was completely satisfied with him even if he had never seen the inside of a decent home. Agrippina was democratic. And Agrippina was the best of all.*

While she may have applauded the moral laxity of her feline friends, in a piece for the *Atlantic* ("The Repeal of Reticence"), she lashed out at sex educators "who—in defiance or in ignorance, of history—believe that evil understood is evil conquered."

"There is nothing new about the Seven Deadly Sins," she wrote. "They are as old as humanity. There is nothing mysterious about them. They are easier to understand than the Cardinal Virtues. Knowledge is the cry. Crude, undigested knowledge, without limit and without reserve. Give it to the girls, give it to the boys, give it to the children."

Agnes Repplier died on December 15, 1950, and after a Solemn High Requiem Mass at Saint John the Evangelist Church on Thirteenth Street in Center City, she was buried in the churchyard. Her obituary stated, "Friends are requested not to send flowers."

PHILADELPHIA'S ONCE-THRIVING PUBLISHING EMPIRE was located in the area of the Curtis Building on Washington Square, which houses artist Maxfield Parrish's famous mural *Dream Garden*. *Dream Garden* came to symbolize how the city's rich publishing history and love of literature and the written word inspired a man named Edward Bok.

In 1887, Bok was an ad manager at *Scribner's* magazine, but two years later he was at the Curtis Building as editor of the *Ladies' Home Journal*. It was Bok who transformed the magazine from a fluffy woman's magazine into a bestselling publication that campaigned for women's suffrage, pacifism and the protection of the environment. Because Bok believed that good art should find a place in public buildings, he asked Cyrus Curtis of Curtis Publishing if he would include a mural in what was then a new structure.

Bok wasn't thinking of the lobby, at least not yet, but of the large public dining room on the building's top floor. He hired Fred Maxfield Parrish to paint a series of seventeen panels between the windows there.

The five-year-long project resulted in panels depicting a series of gardens with youths and maidens frolicking in colorful costumes.

Bok then turned his attention to a large blank white wall in the lobby of the Curtis Building. The wall measured over one thousand square feet. Bok wanted to find another artist, but rather than reemploy Parrish, which would have been the logical thing to do, he looked elsewhere, as if trying to find someone better. He traveled to London and visited with English artist Edwin A. Abbey. Although Abbey was working on a project for the capitol building in Harrisburg, the two men struck a deal. Abbey was given the OK to paint anything he wanted for the Curtis Center. Abbey's idea was a high-minded theme based on *The Grove of Academe*, with Plato and his disciples lounging around in philosophical ecstasy.

Bok returned to America, but the very day that Abbey started the project in London, he fell over dead, as if cursed by a competing artist's voodoo spell.

Bok then went on a talent hunt and found a Wilmington artist named Howard Pyle. Pyle was a good choice because he also happened to know a lot about Plato. But the hoped-for connection never happened because when Bok tried to telephone the artist at his Wilmington home, he was told that Pyle had just died an hour earlier while traveling in Italy.

When a third artist, Boutet de Monvel, a famous decorative master, agreed to do the project, Bok invited de Monvel to Philadelphia to inspect the space at the Curtis Building, but almost immediately after arrangements were made, Monvel died in Paris.

Now it was time for Bok, who was beginning to feel cursed, to take stock. He started to think collectively. He asked six of the leading mural artists in the county to submit full-color mural proposals on any subject of their choosing. The six anonymous submissions were then analyzed by a panel of judges. But this time, the curse manifested itself in the form of six blatant rejections.

He then remembered a glass mosaic curtain by Louis C. Tiffany he'd once seen in Mexico City's Municipal Theatre. He recalled the look of favrile glass set in cement and how that produced a marvelous luminosity. Bok contacted Tiffany and got him to agree to a partnership, but they still needed an artist to provide the preliminary sketch. Bok went back to Parrish and asked him to come up with a sketch for Tiffany despite the fact that Parrish had never worked with glass or mosaics. Parrish's preliminary drawing was approved.

Six months of planning, thirty skilled artisans and over one million pieces of glass later, *Dream Garden* was given a New York exhibition, where it was viewed by over seven thousand people. Art critics at the time were thrilled: they said the mural went way beyond the limited expression of a painted canvas. It took six months for the mural to be disassembled in New York and then reassembled in Philadelphia. In the early twentieth century, almost every home in America had a Maxfield Parrish print. Parrish's work saturated the market. He was Andy Warhol before there was an Andy Warhol. He did covers for *Life*, *Collier's* and *Harper's Weekly* magazines and posters and ads for Hires Root Beer and General Electric. He was commissioned to do murals for office buildings and hotels. In a way, his work—canvases depicting eternal blue skies—reflected the Age of Innocence, although his popularity began to decline in the 1930s. And it really sank after World War II.

CERTAINLY, PHILADELPHIA NOVELIST JOHN T. MCINTYRE, whose first novel, *Steps Going Down*, published in 1936 by Farrar & Rinehart (New York), was familiar with the Curtis Building and the *Dream Garden* mural. McIntyre has always been known as a noir writer, meaning a writer who describes the gritty side of life, as exemplified in the city's underworld. Noir might also be described as the gritty truth underneath a mainstream sugar coating: the life of petty criminals, drug dealers, streetwalkers under the El, small-time mobsters or the unstable drama inside dingy bars filled with cigarette smoke, suspicious characters and, of course, lurking danger.

McIntyre was born in Northern Liberties and left school at age eleven to work full time. For a period, he was a freelance journalist with the *Philadelphia Press*. He wrote over twenty books, most of them noir or crime novels, but some had a conventional slant. A noir novel might also be called "B fiction," as in B movie. One B movie that comes to mind is the 1965 exploitation film *Faster, Pussycat! Kill! Kill!* directed by Russ Meyer and starring Tura Satana. It is about three strippers who wreak havoc and violence on a young couple they encounter in the desert and then kidnap an old, wheelchair-bound man as they attempt to seduce the man's sons for the family money. Although there's some redemption in the fact that all three bad girls come to a bad end, it takes a long time for this to happen.

McIntyre, who was Irish Catholic, manages to weave elements of his Catholicism into the most sordid of his stories. While one chapter may describe how the main character falls in love with a streetwalker, another chapter will present the reader with a small paragraph about the Virgin Mary.

Consider this passage in his novel *Steps Going Down* in which characters Gill and Hogarty are having drinks in a sleazy bar, where "there was noise, and smoke, and the smell of drink in the place…the floor sloppy with spilled beer…the walls grimy with the rubbing of many a loafer's back [as the] cash register rang and rang."[40]

In this section, Gill tells Hogarty that sometimes when he sees what he sees (as in pretty awful stuff), he says a prayer to the Blessed Virgin. "She has a far-reaching voice in Heaven," Gill tells Hogarty. "And God Himself is always hearkening to her. More poor souls have been saved from despair through her than you can put to the credit of all the saints and martyrs in all the far depths of the heavens."[41] As if this nod to religiosity wasn't enough, Gil and Hogarty begin to talk about the Annunciation and the biblical city of Nazareth. But after that, it's a jump to a house of ill repute on Sixteenth Street in Center City.

Curious to know a lot more about McIntyre's life, I headed over to Temple University Archives to examine McIntyre's documents and manuscripts. Oftentimes, when a famous writer dies, his or her papers are turned over to a university. There they are archived and labeled for researchers and biographers. In McIntyre's case, I was able to go through quite a number of boxes. Some of these boxes contained business papers, such as rent receipts, bank correspondence and statements, while others contained personal effects, like personal telephone books, correspondence and rejection letters from publishers.

Although McIntyre published a lot in his lifetime, when he shopped his work around, he got his fair share of bad news. Most of the rejection letters came from the Macmillan Company, a New York publisher. On March 15,

South Philadelphia Market in the style of John T. McIntyre. *Courtesy of the Philadelphia Historical Commission.*

1943, his novel *Gun Smoke Along the Nueces* was turned down. In May of the same year, *Murder in the Mist* was rejected, the letter signed by a Lisa Dwight Cole, an associate editor there. Then, in November, he received a rejection letter for his book *O Land of Milk and Honey*. In 1948, a Macmillan editor sent back his novel *Some Days in the World* and apologized for keeping it so long with the words, "We are very much chagrined at the length of time we have had your manuscript." McIntyre probably rejected the phrase "we are very much chagrined" as a spine-tingling language abomination.

In 1944, McIntyre sent a letter to his friend Alfred Lunt asking for money. McIntyre had just been laid off from a job because business wasn't doing well. He wrote that "just two minutes ago I was told that I was through at Street & Smith's, business conditions being what they are, etc." The letter was painful for me to read because I knew what was coming. "I hate to ask in times like these," McIntyre continues, "but could you possibly send me some money? Every cent I have will be the money I'll get this Friday. We're in damned desperate straits here as it is and this thing will make it just so much worse."

McIntyre ends the letter by requesting "some letters of introduction to men who rate in the publishing business."

One archival box contained an interesting exchange of letters from a Cooperstown, New York banker replying to the novelist's request to purchase back records of a newspaper called the *Saturday Star Journal*. Apparently, McIntyre wanted to know how much the bundle would cost, and the banker put the fee at $300, far too much money for the cash-strapped author, who then offered the banker a counter of $175. The banker replied, "I am not inclined to accept the offer for them of $175 but would be willing to lower my price somewhat. If you wish to make an offer of $225 for the lot, let me know and I will consider it." The exchange was very bureaucratic and unfeeling, the banker obviously looking down at McIntyre from his high financial perch. Then, one month later (March 11, 1941), everything changed. The banker sent a handwritten note to McIntyre refusing the writer's latest offer, but you could feel that something wasn't quite right. Why a handwritten letter? The letters picked up again in August, when the banker sent McIntyre another handwritten note, although it was not on the bank's letterhead. The writing was very disconnected looking and sloppy, as if the writer had a broken hand.

"I went to the hospital April 10th for a severe operation," the banker said. "I am writing to ask you if you are still interested in my *Saturday Star Journals* and if your previous offer for them still holds good. Your offer was $175.00 for the *Star Journals* and $50 for the Dime Libraries." We don't get McIntyre's response, though I imagine he felt some sympathy for the Second National Bank official, who was no longer sounding high and grand. Two weeks later, the two men concluded the deal, and McIntyre got his bundle.

A sad discovery in another box was a 1951 document detailing the writer's funeral expenses from the Oliver Blair Company: "Gray cloth covered casket; silk lining; pillow; old silver extension bar handles; crucifix and services, pine case...$410.00."

RICHARD POWELL's *THE PHILADELPHIAN*, published in 1956 and later made into a film, *The Young Philadelphians*, starring Paul Newman and Robert Vaughn, among others, captures the spirit of the city in its many byzantine subcultures. Powell was the vice-president of one of the largest and oldest advertising agencies in the country, N.W. Ayer & Son, on Washington Square. This seventh-generation Philadelphian once wrote that he would never have started to look "objectively and analytically at Philadelphia if

Philadelphia as it looked to Richard Powell. *Courtesy of Joe Nettis.*

I hadn't worked on a Philadelphia newspaper, and if I hadn't married a girl from Cleveland who began questioning the Philadelphia institutions and beliefs and attitudes which I had accepted as a matter of course."[42]

Some of those attitudes, of course, had to do with the class structure of the city (old families versus immigrant new families, like the Irish). In Powell's novel, we get a simplistic overview of the workings of Philadelphia society:

> *Philadelphia society had long ago worked out a procedure for taking in new members. Money and power were important, but Philadelphia wanted to see if you could produce children and grandchildren who could handle money and power. Marrying well was part of it, but Philadelphia wanted to find out if the blood lines would run true from generation to generation. Proving that you had poise and balance and culture was part of it, but would your children have the same qualities, or would they be freaks and eccentrics? Philadelphia society didn't care for freaks and eccentrics. It had produced very few of them in its two hundred and fifty years of existence.*

The Philadelphian also follows the plight of Irish immigrant Margaret O'Donnell, who arrives in Philadelphia from Ireland in the spring of 1857 and finds employment as a maid with the very Anglo Saxon Protestant Mrs. Clayton, whose husband is a bank official. When poor Margaret becomes pregnant from a one-time roll in the hay with Mrs. Clayton's Harvard law school son, she's quickly told to vacate the premises and paid a handsome sum to care for the baby, a baby the Claytons do not want because of Margaret's station in life.

Mrs. Clayton, however, does visit poor Margaret to assist in the birth of the baby. She does this in a humble city rooming house, where she tells Margaret (in between labor pains), "You're a little Irish bog trotter who thought you could come over here and be a queen. Only it's not that easy."[43] Later, while holding the new baby girl, she tells Margaret one more thing: "You Irish girls with your hot young bodies. As if all you had to do was wave them at a man to get anything you want."[44]

III
THE OVERNIGHT BESTSELLER

No book purporting to be about literary Philadelphia would be complete without a review of the life and career of Christopher Darlington Morley (1890–1957). Like Agnes Repplier, Christopher Morley's life spanned sweeping political changes in Russia and Western Europe, two world wars, the Korean War and even the very beginnings of turmoil in Southeast Asia. The extremely prolific Morley wrote novels, plays, essays and poems. Newspaper columns also flowed from his pen with seemingly careless abandon. In many ways, Morley was a writer's writer with his pipe and sauntering persona, his patrician air and his willingness to listen to almost anybody while on the hunt for a good urban tale.

Born in Bryn Mawr, Pennsylvania, Morley graduated from Haverford College in 1910 and then entered the University of Oxford before taking a job at Doubleday and Company as editor of the *Ladies' Home Journal*, at the time published by Curtis Publishing on Philadelphia's Washington Square. He also became a newspaper columnist for the *Philadelphia Ledger*, which honed his skills for his most famous newspaper column, "Bowling Green," in the *New York Evening Post*.

In New York, where he would go to live with his wife, Helen Booth Fairchild, and his children after six years in Philadelphia, he would help establish the *Saturday Evening Review of Literature* and edit two editions of *Bartlett's Quotations*. When it came to quotations, Morley was never in short supply. "There is only one success, to be able to spend your life in your own way," he wrote—even if, coincidentally, that made a woman or two in his life unhappy, for he also quipped, "A man who has never made a woman angry is a failure in life."

Morley's knowledge of Philadelphia was extensive. In his book *Mince Pie*, he describes his visit to Walt Whitman's house in Camden in an essay entitled "Walt Whitman Miniatures":

> *I don't suppose any literary shrine on earth is of more humble and disregarded aspect than Mickle Street. It is a little cobbled byway, grimed with drifting smoke from the railway yards, littered with wind-blown papers and lined with small wooden and brick houses sooted almost to blackness. It is curious to think, as one walks along that bumpy brick pavement, that many pilgrims from afar have looked forward to visiting Mickle Street as one of the world's most significant altars.*

Explaining the physical peculiarities of Whitman's house, Morley describes it as a "little house, a two-story frame cottage, painted dark brown…On the pavement in front stands a white marble stepping-block with the carved initials W.W.—given to the poet, I dare say, by the same friends who bought him a horse and carriage."

Morley then imagines Whitman coming back from the dead and seeing Philadelphia with new eyes:

> *If Walt could revisit the ferries he loved so well, in New York and Philadelphia, he would find the former strangely altered in aspect. The New York skyline wears a very different silhouette against the sky, with its marvelous peaks and summits drawing the eye aloft. But Philadelphia's profile is (I imagine) not much changed. I do not know just when the City Hall tower was finished: Walt speaks of it as "three-fifths built" in 1879. That, of course, is the dominant unit in the view from Camden. Otherwise there are few outstanding elements. The gradual rise in height of the buildings, from Front Street gently ascending up to Broad, gives no startling contrast of elevation to catch the gaze. The spires of the older churches stand up like soft blue pencils, and the massive cornices of the Curtis and Drexel buildings catch the sunlight. Otherwise the outline is even and well-massed in a smooth ascending curve.*

The essays collected in the volume *Travels in Philadelphia* began as a series of sketches for Morley's column in the *Philadelphia Evening Public Ledger*. Morley called these columns "snapshots of vivacious phases of the life of today." As a resident of the city's Washington Square district, he was a regular habitué of the park benches there and liked to observe the daily goings on. Much like novelist Henry James, who immortalized New York's Washington Square with a novel of the same name, Morley did his best to honor the square in *Travels* when he wrote:

> *And no Walden sky was ever more blue than the roof of Washington Square this morning. Sitting here reading Thoreau I am entranced by the mellow flavor of the young summer. The sun is just goodly enough to set the being in a gentle toasting muse. The trees confer together in a sleepy whisper. I have had buckwheat cakes and syrup for breakfast, and eggs fried both recto and verso; good foundation for speculation. I puff cigarettes and am at peace with myself.*

Although already famous for novels like *Parnassus on Wheels* (1917), *The Haunted Bookshop* (1919) and *Thunder on the Left* (1925), it would be the novel *Kitty Foyle* (1939) that would catapult his career into the mainstream eye. The "shocking for its day" story of a young working-class Philadelphia girl who falls in love with a young socialite while striving for a career

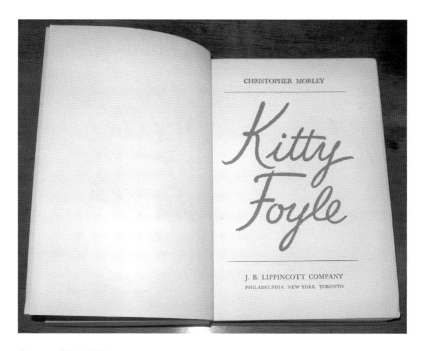

Courtesy of Joe McClernan.

in business was unorthodox enough, but with the added caveat of a pregnancy out of wedlock followed by an abortion, it blew the collective factory whistles of disapproving critics. Despite the controversy, the success of the book brought worldwide recognition to Philadelphia's J.B. Lippincott, the book's publishing house. In 1940, the bestselling novel became a film directed by Philadelphia-born Sam Wood and starring Ginger Rogers. Advertisements for the film read: "A Natural History of a Woman...And Her Two Men."

Throughout his life, Morley corresponded with noted writers and figures of the time, including Carl Sandburg, T.S. Eliot, Joseph Conrad, Sherwood Anderson, Pearl S. Buck and Hilaire Belloc. The wide variety of his correspondents lends credibility to his advice to readers to "read, every day, something no one else is reading. Think, every day, something no one else is thinking. Do, every day, something no one else would be silly enough to do. It is bad for the mind to continually be part of unanimity."

In Roslyn Estates, New York, Morley hand built a cabin or hermitage that became his writing studio. It was here that he wrote his autobiography and edited works by other writers and where he worked until the end of his life. He died in 1957 after a number of strokes.

WHILE MORLEY'S PHILADELPHIA WAS "a surprisingly large town at the confluence of the Biddle and Drexel families...wholly surrounded by cricket teams, fox hunters, beagle packs, and the Pennsylvania Railroad," novelist James Michener's world was more of a shantytown experience approaching the rustic atmosphere of Appalachia.

Born on February 3, 1907, Michener was raised by Mabel Michener, whose husband, Edwin, had died five years before his birth. In the many interviews about his life, the author of *Chesapeake* and *Hawaii* claimed he never knew who his father was. While biographers and critics speculate about who fathered Michener, most categorize the writer as a foundling who was brought up in such poverty that he had to fight his brothers in order to get his share of food. It didn't help that Mabel had a tendency to adopt abandoned kids, which made for tight living quarters all around. Despite the family's poverty, Mabel read to her children every night from the works of Dickens, Twain and Thackeray. This experience certainly gave Michener an edge when it came to the appreciation of literature.

By age fourteen, Michener had read the complete works of Balzac—no small task, especially when one considers that only a few years before he was a regular habitué at the local five-cent Saturday serials that ran in fifteen-week theater installments. It was these movie serials that first got him thinking about becoming a writer. There can be little doubt that Mabel's nightly reading sessions also helped him win a full scholarship to Swarthmore College, from which he graduated summa cum laude. Michener was anything but an average college student, however; before he was a freshman, he had embarked on a life of adventure and intrigue and became, in a sense, a Bucks County version of Jack Kerouac when he hitchhiked across the nation and even rode the rails hobo style from Canada to Mexico. His many odd jobs at that time included a stint as an amusement park worker, where he saw his fair share of bloodshed, including the murder of drifters and prostitutes behind the tents and the trailer homes bordering the circus.[45]

After college, Michener taught school before enlisting in the navy during World War II, although his Quaker upbringing prevented him from joining as a combatant. In the South Pacific, he began writing stories about the life he found there, namely on themes having to do with racial relationships, such as the fate of an upper-class lieutenant when he had an affair with a native girl and the drama surrounding a naval nurse's marriage to a French planter. At the war's conclusion, Michener consolidated these stories into a volume he titled *Tales of the South Pacific*. The book went on to win the Pulitzer Prize for Literature, eventually becoming the basis for the Richard Rodgers and Oscar Hammerstein Broadway hit musical *South Pacific*. Michener saw his South Pacific experience as life changing and saw himself as the last in a line of a number of world-class writers, like Melville, Conrad and Maughn, who have written about the South Pacific. The eighteen loosely connected stories in *Tales of the South Pacific*, Michener says, almost wrote themselves. "I did little corrections. The chapters arranged themselves—it almost wrote itself."[46]

Michener's thousand-page books are generally noted for their darker view of history. Critics have noticed that his epic novels generally follow a standard template: there's a concentration on a piece of land or country; then his novelist's eye focuses on the original inhabitants of that land, their culture and habits; and then the story unfolds to the present day. Throughout his lifetime, Michener's epics were usually overnight bestsellers before they even reached the bookstores. As a working writer, his habit was to move to the area that he was writing about and then remain in that area until the book was finished. Michener's bestselling formula for writing epic novels, of course, stopped at the shores of nonfiction. His nonfiction books *Literary Reflections* and *The World Is My Home: A Memoir*, his 1992 autobiography, are favorites with readers who might not necessarily be fans of his novels. Published in

1941, *Literary Reflections* is about the famous authors and personalities who helped shape and influence Michener, who in every sense of the word can be called a survivor:

> *I survived three airplane wrecks, three bar room brawls, three marriages, a riot in Saigon, a near-going in the streets of Pamplona, a cable car I was in was struck by lightning in Buenos Aires, and I once got hit in the face with a line drive in baseball when I thought I was dead.*[47]

Into every public life, a few controversies often creep; certainly this was true for the Doylestown-born writer. At the height of his fame, he created a major controversy in Philadelphia when he wrote in a *Holiday* magazine feature in 1950 that West Manayunk, just across the river from Philadelphia's Manayunk neighborhood, was "Lower Merion Township's dark closet." Michener's "dark closet" reference, of course, conjured up a leper colony, an undesirable place or a shantytown. Given Michener's international reputation, West Manayunk schoolchildren were soon seen as social outcasts. In his article, Michener wrote that along the Lower Merion Schuylkill waterfront, a "somewhat impoverished citizenry lives clinging to the river's edge…the Cliffside town of West Manayunk perches Pittsburgh-like in the gloom." One cannot blame the writer for offering an honest rendering of what he felt to be the truth, but for West Manayunkers, seeing the truth in print was too much to bear.

In response, they organized town meetings and even arranged a debate between Michener and Dr. Albert C. Barnes of the Barnes Foundation. The cantankerous Dr. Barnes, himself an outcast from Philadelphia society, was the first to challenge Michener. It didn't help that Barnes, who hated intellectuals, was still annoyed that Michener had once impersonated a steelworker in order to be admitted to his museum, since he did not allow anyone he thought an intellectual to be admitted to his gallery, the Barnes Foundation, at that time in Merion, Pennsylvania. But the dye from the *Holiday* magazine article had been cast. In October 1953, the West Manayunk Civic Association asked residents to vote on the existing name or one of four alternatives. Of the total 896 votes, 475 chose Belmont Hills, while 269 favored the old name of West Manayunk.

Before his death on October 17, 1997, Michener had been married three times. In 1935, he married Patti Koon; in 1948, he was the husband of Vange Nord; and his last marriage to Mari Yoriko ended in 1994 with her death.

Manayunk Canal. *Courtesy of John Kiker.*

On October 17, 1997, the *New York Times* announced that "James Michener, Author of Novels That Sweep Through the History of Places, Is Dead." The obituary came nine years after one of Michener's fondest wishes from the 1960s came true: the opening of a regional art museum, the James A. Michener Art Museum in Doylestown, in September 1988. Doylestown's most famous son was now part of the area's physical landscape.

IN 1941, NOVELIST CHRISTOPHER ISHERWOOD was working with the Quakers during World War II and spent some time on Philadelphia's Main Line. In his diaries of the period, Isherwood notes that while taking the train to Haverford station, "my first impression…was that all the people in the coach belonged to one of three or four distinctly recognizable families." Isherwood explains that his perception may have been based on the contrast between homogeneous Pennsylvania and Los Angeles's ever-changing, diverse population: "The men were tall, bony, big shouldered, fair haired and quite nice looking, but somehow fatally 'pithed,' as though the marrow had been drained from their bones." Isherwood goes on to to say that they had an air of quiet anxiety:

They spoke slowly, prudently, selecting their words from a small, odd vocabulary. The women were bright and energetic. They used no makeup, and their white skin was dotted with freckles. They had sandy gold hair, dragged back and twisted into a knot. The country we were passing couldn't possibly have been less "my sort": it was tame, suburban, pretty, a landscape without secrets. [48]

Like the rolling hills of Bucks County around Doylestown, the Malvern-Bacton Hill area of Chester County has its own attractions, especially when it comes to farms. While the farm of writer Daniel P. Mannix IV may not have been a conventional farm, it became a legend in the Philadelphia area because it served as a kind of zoo with a collection of exotic animals. As an adventure writer, Mannix traveled the world with his wife, Jule Junker Mannix, in search of cheetahs, llamas, spider monkeys, a python and even a small elephant to raise at their Bacton Hill property.

After his birth on October 27, 1911, Daniel P. Mannix IV, the son of American naval officer Daniel P. Mannix III, embarked on a highly unconventional life that included youthful stints as a circus sideshow performer, a magician and a trainer of eagles. These experiences helped him become the author of more than twenty-five books, including stories on big game hunting, a biography of occultist Aleister Crowley and what is perhaps the best animal story of all time, *The Fox and the Hound*, an unsentimental tale about a fox and a hound in the wild from the animals' points of view. The book is about animals in their own environment and seems far removed from the syrupy landscape of the Walt Disney film of the same name, adapted from the book but which bears little resemblance to Mannix's original story.

I met Mannix as a high school student when the author's son, Danny, a classmate of mine, brought me into his father's book-lined study. Dressed in a Harris Tweed jacket and smoking a pipe, Mannix was sitting by a window that had a commanding view of the zoo, although no animals were visible to me then. Smoke billowed from the writer's pipe like steam from a vintage locomotive.

I don't remember whether I was introduced to Peter the Python, the author's most dangerous exotic pet, but I did see a snake or two.

In his autobiography *My Life with All Creatures Great and Small*, Mannix has a few words to say about Peter the Python. "Handling a big snake," he wrote, "is an unforgettable experience. There is the gentle touch of the soft lips and delicate tongue, together with the strange feeling that you are holding a living electric current swathed in smooth scales."

Mannix also reminds readers that pythons are not poisonous: "Peter, like all constrictors, kills by wrapping his coils around his victim, usually a chicken or a rabbit."[49]

Pythons, Mannix continues, rarely kill human beings because "a man has hands and can generally unwrap a snake before he loses consciousness." The Mannix family allowed Peter to slither around the house, and Peter, being a semiaquatic creature, would curl up near the plumbing in the bathroom or, worse yet, go inside the toilet for a long, cozy nap.

"Peter strongly disliked having the toilet flush when he was inside," Mannix wrote, adding that when that happened, he would rise up and give one of his long, loud hisses.

As for the houseguest who inadvertently sat on the bowl with Peter inside, that's another story.

Mannix's first book was *The Backyard Zoo*, about the family's eclectic collection of pets. After this came *More Backyard Zoo*. Mannix also wrote about his experiences as a side show act working in carnivals. He incorporated his experiences as a sword swallower, fire-eater, trainer of wild animals and magician, known as the Great Zadma, into his bestselling books.

Daniel P. Mannix. *Courtesy of Julie Mannix von Zerneck and Daniel P. Mannix V.*

In *Memoirs of a Sword Swallower*, he describes carnival life when he tells stories about the Fat Lady, the human beanpole and the Ostrich Man who ate broken glass.

In *Freaks*, Mannix describes the love affairs of little people (called midgets in those days); the story of elephant boy; the amours of Jolly Daisy, the fat woman; the notorious pinhead who inspired Verdi's *Rigoletto*; and the black little person, only thirty-four inches tall, who was very happily married to a 264-pound woman. Then there was the human torso with a talent for sewing and typing.

Freaks, as one reviewer wrote, comprises "bizarre accounts of normal humans turned into freaks—either voluntarily or by evil design!"

Mannix's early books contain photographs from the 1930s and '40s (all taken by the author) that memorialize the goings on in the forgotten world of circus performance artists.

In *The Beast: The Scandalous Life of Aleister Crowley*, Mannix writes about the English occultist and ceremonial magician. After the book was released, Mannix received an invitation to join Anton LaVey's Church of Satan, but he refused the offer since LaVey obviously couldn't distinguish between the curious and sometimes sensationalist imagination of the writer versus the world of personal belief.

Mannix was still a member of our local Catholic parish, and it was not unusual to see him and Jule receive Communion on Sundays. A serious LaVey connection would have meant the end of the author's weekly Mass attendance.

Mannix's most famous book, *Those About to Die*, takes the reader into the bowels of the Roman games in the Coliseum and into the daily lives of gladiators. This book was reprinted in 2001 as *The Way of the Gladiator* and became the inspiration for the 2000 movie *Gladiator*.

Mannix published *The Hellfire Club* about the secret decorated caves in England where the country's once-famous "1 percenters" engaged in parliamentary-style meetings and various forms of sexual debauchery. Eminent and respected men from the worlds of arts, letters and politics, including Benjamin Franklin, were said to be habitués of these dens of vice where everything was permitted.

Mannix, who died in 1997 at age eighty-five, survived his wife, Jule, by twenty years.

Today, there's a renewed interest in his work, as many of his earlier out-of-print books have been republished. While I have not revisited the Chester County zoo where the young Liz Taylor was once said to have stayed while filming *National Velvet*, I did discover that Mannix had once partnered with

Daniel P. Mannix. *Courtesy of Julie Mannix von Zerneck and Daniel P. Mannix V.*

famed literary critic Malcolm Cowley when they coauthored *The Middle Passage*, a disturbing essay that focuses on the mechanics of slavery, its origins in Africa, its European history and what happened on the slave ships that came to America.

We learn, for instance, that "the vast majority of the Negroes brought to America had been enslaved and sold to the whites by other Africans." These other Africans "were coastal tribes and states, like Efik kingdom of Calabar, that based their whole economy on the slave trade."

The authors report that the slaves might have been prisoners of war, kidnapped by groups of black marauders or even sold with their entire

Daniel P. Mannix. *Courtesy of Julie Mannix von Zerneck and Daniel P. Mannix V.*

families for such "high" crimes as adultery, impiety or, as the authors state, "stealing a tobacco pipe."

Slaves were shackled two by two and then sent below the ship, although female slaves were allowed to roam the vessel so that the sailors could see which ones they could have their way with. Mannix writes, "All the slaves were forced to sleep without covering on bare wooden floors…In a stormy passage the skin over their elbows might be worn away to the bare bone."

In the morning, the sailors would oversee the "dancing of the slaves," a ritual in which the chained slaves would be forced to dance around the deck by the cat-o-nine-tail-armed sailors. This happened while one slave pounded a drum or a sailor played a bagpipe. This therapeutic ritual was a precaution against "suicidal melancholy," although the authors report that many slaves suffered from a condition known as "fixed melancholy," an expression used to describe a state when a slave had lost the will to live, despite being well cared for.

Diseases like yellow fever plagued these ships, as did the smell of human excrement, which could be detected miles away, depending on air currents.

Mutinies were not uncommon given the conditions on board. Sometimes the ship's crew would be slaughtered, although then the problem for the slaves became where to dock the ship because, at least for them, there was no such thing as freedom.[50]

ASTUTE WRITERS, IT IS SAID, should learn to be on guard when it comes to the subject of literary critics.

Consider what one editor wrote to Emily Dickinson in 1862, when he rejected one of her poems: "Queer—the rhymes were all wrong."[51]

Or what another editor told Flaubert when he rejected *Madame Bovary* in 1856 with the comment, "You have buried your novel underneath a heap of details."[52]

Or what about the rejection letter received by William Faulkner in 1931 for his novel *Sanctuary*: "Good God, I can't publish this."[53]

When Pearl S. Buck submitted *The Good Earth* to one publisher in 1931, she was told that it could not be published because "the American public is not interested in anything on China." *The Good Earth*, though not the author's first book, became a critical and popular success despite the conviction of the critic who thought the book would bore American readers. Buck wrote *The Good Earth* in three months after the birth of her mentally retarded daughter, Carol, because she wanted to have enough money to support her. In 1932, she was awarded the Pulitzer Prize for *The Good Earth*; the Nobel Prize for Literature followed in 1938 for her genuine portrayals of Chinese life. The Nobel Prize announcement shocked writers like Theodore Dreiser, John Dos Passos and Ernest Hemingway because they felt that they were more deserving of the honor. *The Good Earth* went on to become the second all-time bestseller of the twentieth century, second only to *Gone With the Wind*.

The post-Nobel Buck also had to contend with choruses of critics pointing fingers. "Mrs. Buck is unrepresentative of American letters," they said. "Her work in no way reflects the literary and ideological ferment of 20th Century." The high-handed insult stung, but Buck seemed to take it in stride. "Like the Chinese," she said in her Nobel Prize address, "I have been taught to write for these people." She meant "these people" as opposed to an intellectual elite. She was not, as some might have wished, an early Presbyterian version of Susan Sontag.

"'The Good Earth,'" said journalist Edgar Snow, "was the first book that made western countries conscious of the Far East."[54]

Pearl S. Buck. *Courtesy of Pearl S. Buck International.*

Born Pearl Sydenstricker in 1892 in West Virginia to Southern Presbyterian missionary parents, at three months old she was taken to China, where she would spend the next forty years, barring a sojourn in the United States when she went to a women's college in Lynchburg, Virginia. She returned to China in 1914 after graduation and met John Lossing Buck. The two were married in 1917 and had a daughter, Carol, who was born with severe mental retardation. In 1925, Pearl returned to the United States to obtain a master's degree in English at Cornell University. But it was the situation with Carol that plunged Pearl into a depression, and for a time, she consulted specialists and doctors in the hopes that Carol could be helped. Buck wrote in her autobiography, *For Spacious Skies*, that she achieved a sense of peace when a specialist told her that her daughter's condition would never change:

> *Listen to what I tell you! I tell you, Madame, the child can never be normal. Do not deceive yourself. You will wear out your life and beggar your family unless you give up hope and face the truth. She will never be well…She will never be able to speak properly. She will never be more than about four years old, at best. Prepare yourself…I tell you the truth for you own sake.*

After Pearl found an institution for Carol, she and John began adopting children in 1925. Their eighteen-year marriage was not a happy one, although it was during this period that Pearl began to amass the material she would use in *The Good Earth*. She had already published her first book, *East Wind, West Wind*, in 1930 and was writing stories for *Asia* magazine and *Atlantic Monthly*. Her marital unhappiness would end after the 1931 publication of *The Good Earth*, when the book's publisher, William Walsh of Paul Dry Books, and she became close friends. In 1934, she and Walsh would move to the United States and were married the following year. With Carol safely institutionalized in New Jersey, Pearl was now free to adopt six more children with her new husband. She then bought a large old farmhouse in Bucks County and went on to write seventy books, including novels, collections of stories, poetry and children's literature.

After *The Good Earth*, she wrote *Sons*, a tale of sons rising against their fathers as revolutionary winds swept through China. The book was viewed as a critical success; many, in fact, saw it as superior to *The Good Earth*. Several other novels would follow. But after years of working and living in obscurity, Buck found her newfound fame difficult to handle. As Peter J. Conn notes in his study on the author, *Pearl S. Buck: A Cultural Biography* (1998):

> *Pearl had decidedly mixed feelings about her new found fame. She had spent too many years in the shadows to feel comfortable in the light. More to the point, she mistrusted her own talent. Although she pretended to be indifferent to hostile opinion, she was sensitive to condescension that she suffered at the hands of the serious quarterlies and advanced taste makers.*

In a 1958 Mike Wallace television interview with the author, Wallace starts the questioning in true 1950s fashion by announcing, "The battle between the sexes is a major social problem."

"Yes," Pearl Buck answers. "Most women make their home their graves."

Wallace is perplexed, even annoyed, by the comment.

"It's difficult to understand how women make their home their graves," he says, to which Buck replies, "I think because they stop reading books that would enlarge their minds or their family's minds."

"It's also difficult to be an American," Buck adds. "We're committed to loneliness."

"I don't get it," Wallace confesses.

"Well, you know, the old countries have a tradition of family and church support, so there's less choices there. Americans don't have traditional support

Pearl S. Buck. *Courtesy of Pearl S. Buck International.*

systems that Europeans have. They live in a country with no boundaries and no patterns."

When her autobiography, *For Spacious Skies* (1966), written in collaboration with Theodore F. Harris, was published, Buck appeared on *The Merv Griffin Show* and explained to the talk show host her feelings about Communism in China. Communism, she said, is "a curious impossible, impractical scheme of life; it's not based on anything that's sound psychologically…the Chinese are marvelous friends and frightful enemies."

Pearl Buck died from lung cancer in Vermont in 1973, although she is buried on the grounds of her estate, now the Pearl S. Buck Foundation, an organization the author founded in 1964.

When most people think of the Pearl S. Buck House, they think of the sprawling sixty-acre estate in Bucks County. But long before the women's rights crusader, philanthropist, humanitarian and author moved to this house (or Green Hills Farm), she lived at 2019 Delancey Street in Center City.

The Delancey Street house, despite its having been occupied by the famous author of over seventy books and the winner of the 1938 Nobel Prize for Literature for *The Good Earth*, was built in 1860 in the humble Federal style, and in 1918, the multiple-dwelling row house was later recast in the Beaux Arts style by the Philadelphia architectural firm of DeArmond, Ashmead & Bickley.

DeArmond, Ashmead & Bickley (1911–1938), all University of Pennsylvania graduates, were famous for their Colonial Revival residences and English-influenced-style buildings.

Ms. Buck's Delancey Street town house and the Christmas season go together. It was in this Center City house where Ms. Buck compiled her 1972 short story collection, *Once Upon a Christmas*. The Christmas season, in fact, figures in a lot of Ms. Buck's children's stories. Stories like "Christmas Miniature" (1957), "The Christmas Ghost" (1960) and "Christmas Day in the Morning," in which an impoverished son searches for the perfect gift for his father on Christmas Eve, may also have been written in the Delancey Street town house.

Pearl S. Buck's estate. *Courtesy of Pearl S. Buck International.*

The nine-thousand-square-foot, five-floor town house was purchased in 1964 as the home of Pearl Buck and the Pearl S. Buck Foundation. While the basement and first floor were renovated for use as foundation space, the second floor was designed to house the dining room, a formal drawing room and the solarium or sun room where Buck had large numbers of plants.

With the famous Rosenbach Museum and Library just a few doors away at 2010 Delancey Street, it's no wonder that Buck saw this area as a special part of Center City. It may have been the beginning of the tumultuous '60s,

The Pearl S. Buck Center City town house. *Author's collection.*

but in those days Pearl Buck was referred to as "Miss Buck," and it is said that she dressed like a society matron, while in her Bucks County home she was far more informal.

The octagonal-shaped dining room was lavishly decorated with a Ming screen with inlaid ivory figures. A long Chinese buffet table was also situated under a smoked glass mirror. Since the dining room also doubled as a place for dancing, the octagonal table could be rolled into a closet, and the chandelier could be raised or lowered as needed.

"Why did I choose Center City, you ask?" Pearl S. Buck once wrote. "Because there was a street, there was the house, there were the people. There, too, was the tradition of brotherly love." Buck also wrote that no matter where she lived, there were always elements of the Chinese: "Sooner or later into every room in any house I own the Chinese influence creeps."

At 2019 Delancey Street, the third-floor library contained a baby grand piano, the famous "Good Earth Desk" and an ancient Chinese drum on a pedestal that acted as a coffee table, as well as leather-bound editions of her books given to her as gifts by her publisher. Much of the furniture was imported from the Buck house in China, namely the rose and tan Peking rugs, the blackwood chairs and a daybed.

The third-floor master bedroom had a small sitting room and a writing table.

One walked through the first-floor entryway into a vestibule that exploded with red lacquered doors, stained glass and a large statue of the Chinese Goddess of Mercy. Beyond the foyer, near the fireplace with its Mandarin Chinese chairs, was an altar table flanked by two antique candelabra.

During the renovation of the town house in 1964–65, the first-floor kitchen was moved to the basement, and the former kitchen became the foundation's conference room. In the center of the conference room was a six-foot round table made of walnut and yellow marble.

Many of Buck's Delancey Street town house treasures were moved to the Bucks County home when the town house was sold.

FOR A WRITER, THE ABILITY TO ENTERTAIN readers doesn't require a pronounced accent or a certain pose while smoking a pipe. Raw talent can appear anywhere. It can even assume the guise of the so-called average man in a pickup truck. Take Philly's Pete Dexter, for instance. Dexter is about as far from the "finely cultured" literary gentleman as one can get. In personal appearances and in interviews about his astonishing writing career, he usually appears in a baseball cap (sometimes cocked at an angle), his hair uneven and spiraling out from behind his ears like a country boy.

In YouTube interviews, Dexter doesn't appear to be as tall as the people who interview him. I noticed something else about the man: he has eyes like Edgar Allan Poe. Poe, of course, had a highly dramatic personal life. Dexter's life, especially when he lived in Philly, was also highly dramatic.

Like Poe, Dexter didn't make Philly his permanent home. He was born in Pontiac, Michigan, in 1943; did his undergrad work at the University of South Dakota; and eventually wound up in Philly because of journalism, arriving just before Christmas 1974 to turn out articles for the *Philadelphia Daily News*. Before that, the Puget Sound, Washington resident worked a series of menial jobs like mail sorter in a post office, car salesman and truck driver. He was once even a ditch digger in Florida. This was before he landed his first job in journalism as a novice reporter for the *South Florida Sun-Sentinel*. He lucked out one day when he saw a Help Wanted ad for a reporter in the window of the *Sentinel* office, something that would never happen in today's world. He got the job and after that worked as a reporter for the *Palm Beach Post*. He also started writing for magazines, but his real jump into the newspaper limelight occurred when he began working for the *Philadelphia Daily News*.

By the time he left Philly in 1986, he was easily the city's most famous columnist, but it would be two years after his arrival here in 1974 before *Daily News* editor Gil Spencer would let him try his hand at writing a column. Dexter hasn't always gotten along with newspaper editors. There's a famous story about how he once threatened to push an editor's head into a pot of chili during a holiday party.[55]

These were the days when newspaper columnists produced two or three columns a week at eight to nine hundred words per column. Newspaper columnists today appear once a week, if they are lucky. Dexter likes to say that columnists who are published once a week can easily hide who they are, but when you write three, four or five times a week, you can't hide who you are from readers. "A pose exposes itself," he says.[56]

Dexter likes to joke and say that he got his column at the *Daily News* because the editors there got tired of him pestering them about writing stories. But once he settled into the life of a columnist, he says it was one of the happiest periods of his life. His Philly column-writing days were fun and reckless. He could be seen hanging out (and closing out) bars like Dirty Frank's, McGlinchey's and Doc Watson's in Center City. He had a penchant for pushing the envelope, getting into small fights, wrecking company cars and carousing into the wee hours.

Then there was his fateful column on December 9, 1981, about the efforts to combat drug dealing in the tough, often violent Irish neighborhood of Grays Ferry, called Devil's Pocket, near Center City. Entitled "In Tasker, It's About to Stop," the column mentioned the death of a twenty-one-year-old guy. After the column was published, Dexter got a call from the dead man's mother, angry that he had called her son a doper in print. The dead man's brother, a bartender in Grays Ferry, was also on the line with the mother, demanding that Dexter retract everything he wrote. Dexter refused to do that but said that he might go to the bar and have a chat with the bartender to iron things out.

The column began, "A couple of weeks ago, a kid named Buddy Lego was found dead in Cobbs Creek. It was a Sunday afternoon. He was from the neighborhood, a good athlete, a nice kid. Stoned all the time. The kind of kid you think you could have saved."

When Dexter went to the bar, he introduced himself to the bartender and then made it clear that he still wasn't going to retract anything. At this point, the scenario gets fuzzy. Dexter says that somebody hit him from behind, knocking out or "shaving down" some of his teeth; later reports have the bartender attacking him with the cue stick. Dazed and bloodied, the columnist went home and contacted his prizefighter friend Randall "Tex" Cobb and a few others, and then they all decided to go back to Dougherty's to protect Dexter during his second attempt to "reason" with the bartender.

But as soon as they entered the bar, Dexter has said in interviews that a fat, ugly red-haired guy ran out and then came back with numerous men with tire irons, nightsticks and a baseball bat. Since you cannot reason with tigers, sometimes the only thing to do is strike while the iron is hot, but for Dexter, Cobb and friends it was too late to defend themselves and spring into action. There were just too many people to fight.

The thirty-eight-year-old columnist was out cold on the sidewalk, and Cobb had been injured as well. The rest of the group took off. Dexter had a broken pelvis, bleeding on the brain, a concussion and plenty of nerve damage to his hands. But his troubles were just beginning. During surgery, there had been a problem with the anesthesia so that, while it appeared he was totally out—meaning mute and unable to move—he could feel the surgeon drilling into his leg but was unable to do anything about it. What saved the day was the fact that his heart was beating furiously; after that, he was numbed sufficiently.[57]

Dexter says that the horrendous pain he felt would have driven a lot of people to the nut house. While recovering from the incident, he started work on his first novel, *God's Pocket*.

The incident would pave the way for his move to Sacramento from Philly. In 1986, he wrote his last column for the *Daily News*:

> *I have seen a pope. I have seen Julius Erving at the top of his game. I have seen a city administrator burn down a neighborhood. I watched Randall Cobb slowly realize he would never become heavyweight champion of the world. One night I almost watched myself die. And as moving as those things were at the time, they are not what endure. What endures are the people I loved. Somewhere along the line, this city has done me a profound favor. I glimpse it once in a while at night in the street, among the people who live there, or along the road. Hitchhikers. It cuts fresh every time. I recognize the lost faces because one of them, I think, was supposed to be mine.*

In Sacramento, he started a new life as a columnist for the *Sacramento Bee* and then proceeded to write a series of groundbreaking novels, beginning with *Deadwood* in 1986; *Paris Trout*, 1988, which won the 1988 U.S. National Book Award; *Brotherly Love*, 1991; *The Paperboy*, 1995; *Train*, 2003; and *Spooner*, 2009. Dexter has been called "a tough son of a bitch with the kind heart of a natural humorist." The author of some twelve novels also had three of his best newspaper columns appear in *Deadline Artists: America's Greatest Newspaper Columns*, which included the works of Jimmy Breslin, Will Rogers and Walter Lippmann.

His years as a columnist paid off because when he'd work on his novels, he would write two pages or nine hundred words per day. He likes to say that his books are pretty dark, but he also says that he doesn't "walk around like that all the time." His novel *Spooner* has been compared to Thomas Wolfe's *Look Homeward, Angel* and even the works of Mark Twain. It's not often that you hear the name Thomas Wolfe these days. Of course, it was the very tall Wolfe who used to write in longhand on long yellow legal tablets while standing up and using the top of his refrigerator as a desktop. Wolfe would then take the completed manuscript—meaning boxes of these legal tablets filled with his cursive scribble—into the office of his editor, Maxwell Perkins of Charles Scribner's Sons, New York, who would then hand it to a secretary to type out.

Dexter likes to write at night, when it is quiet. He writes everyday, unlike some writers who can go for weeks and even months at a time without writing anything. Regarding *Spooner*, Dexter says that he hates the word "memoir," adding that the novel is "more true than a memoir would have been" and that the story "kind of follows a lot of the places, characters, and events in my life." This includes the characterization of his stepfather, whom Dexter says he keeps dreaming about and to whom he dedicated his first book, *Deadwood*. In *Spooner*, there's a saintly character named Calmer, an old South Dakota name, who in many ways represents the figure of his stepfather.[58] In Dexter's fourth novel, *Brotherly Love*, about a power-hungry union boss with Mafia connections, the staccato prose style is reminiscent of the feel of a screenplay. The novel captures the underbelly thug culture of the world of roofers and amateur Mafioso. The prose is not for the fainthearted:

> *A week to the day after Bobby is left in a garbage bag on the service road at the airport, Michael climbs through the kitchen window of a small brick tow house on Snyder Avenue—Leonard Crawley boosting him up, Monk already waiting inside—and takes the old Italian who lives there out of his bed, a confused old man who cannot see them without his glasses, and tapes him to the water heater in the basement. His wife finds him there, his socks sticking halfway out of his mouth, when she comes back from Levittown. She has been there visiting her grandchildren. The bats they used, stained with the old man's blood, are still lying on the basement floor. Peter reads the details of the old man's death in the* Daily News. *It says he was naked.*

When writing a novel, Dexter says he has the feeling that he is not in control: "When I start a book it's usually with just a character in mind, something small and then I feel like I'm an observer, watching things. The book goes its own direction, don't try to steer it...I'm not one of those people who outline plots."

Dexter believes that writers should write to entertain audiences—"If not, what is it for?" he asks—but agrees that it's impossible to predict the marketplace or what the public will like. In one interview, he comes down hard on Dan Brown, who "sells a billion books, but can't write a line." Dexter says he's never walked into an airport or an airplane and seen somebody reading one of his books, whereas he's seen people reading Dan Brown.[59]

His encounter with the Philly thugs in the Devil's Pocket marked him for life. The experience changed his taste perception; alcohol, for instance, now tastes like battery acid to him, so he sticks to just an occasional beer when he goes out with his wife, Dian. He says he doesn't miss Philly when it comes to the traffic and the noise and waiting in line. "People don't realize how much of their lives they spend doing that stuff."

"The perfect life," he says, would be to transport himself to Philly for three hours a day, get that soft pretzel and then leave.

ON THE MONEYED SIDE OF the literary landscape, where baseball caps are relegated to the suburban toolshed, is Buzz Bissinger, nonfiction writer, columnist for the *Beast* and a contributing editor of *Vanity Fair*. The Pulitzer Price–winning journalist and author is best known for his book *Friday Night Lights: A Town, a Team, and a Dream*, the story of a Texas high school football team during its 1988 season. Bissinger often writes about sports. In 2005, he penned *Three Nights in August*, a *New York Times* bestseller that documented the trials and tribulations of the St. Louis Cardinals and the Chicago Cubs in 2003. In 2009, his star faded somewhat with the publication of *Shooting Stars*, about basketball star LeBron James. Bissinger says he wrote this book for money and prefers to forget that he wrote it. It would have been easy for him to typecast himself as a sportswriter, especially after *Sports Illustrated* called *Friday Night Lights* the best book on football, but Bissinger's interests are too vast for a sports-only mode.

Harry Gerard "H.G" Bissinger III was born in November 1954 and educated at Philips Academy and the University of Pennsylvania. At Penn, he was an editor at the *Daily Pennsylvanian*, later going on to write for the *Philadelphia Inquirer*, where he won a Pulitzer for his investigation of the Philadelphia court system. His 1998 feature article in *Vanity Fair*, "Shattered Glass," about the writing career of disgraced *New Republic* writer Stephen Glass, was the basis for the 2003 film of the same name.

His one political book was the 1998 *Prayer for the City*, in which he followed Philadelphia mayor Ed Rendell's first campaign. A much more personal and therapeutic book for Bissinger was *Father's Day: A Journey into the Mind and Heart of My Extraordinary Son*, which took him four years to write and which forced him to confront many of his personal demons having to do with his son Zach's mental disabilities. In *Father's Day*, Bissinger attempts to exorcise the emotional pain caused by birth complications surrounding Zach's premature birth. That premature birth caused Zach to have the mentality of a nine-year-old, although his son would exhibit a strange talent for matching up random dates with the correct day of the week. Zach, then, is a kind of savant, but Bissinger at odd times has called his son "mentally retarded" and even expressed disappointment that Zach can work only odd jobs that involve physical labor and materials. "It shames me to think," he has said, "my son's professional destiny is paper or plastic."

Father's Day is an account of a ten-day cross-country road trip that Bissinger took with Zach and his twin brother, Gerry (he has another son, Caleb, from his second marriage). The book is an in-depth Norman Mailer–like examination of his relationship to the twins but especially to Zach. Some reviewers have praised the book, while others expressed the thought that they wished the book was "less Buzz and more Zach."

"As much as I try to engage Zach, figure out how to make the flower germinate because there is a seed, I also run. I run out of guilt," Bissinger writes in *Father's Day*. "I run because he was robbed and I feel I was robbed. I run because of my shame. I am not proud to feel or say this. But I think these things, not all the time, but too many times, which only increases the cycle of my shame. This is my child. How can I look at him this way? "

The author then recounts a shopping trip with Zach to Brooks Brothers on Philadelphia's Walnut Street:

He comes out of the dressing room. The pants cannot make it over his protruding stomach. The legs billow like the jib of a sailboat in a dead wind. I silently rail against the cruelty of his metabolism that in a few years has made his midsection mushroom after being stick thin throughout his youth. The salesman knows I am trying to dress this man-child in Brooks Brothers from head to toe. He intuits my need to keep alive some fantasy that my son must have gray flannels because he works as a lawyer or hedge fund trader...We purchase the blazer, which Zach is still wearing. He asks the salesman if they have a pocket square he could put into the breast pocket because that's what my uncle wears and maybe it would be nice maybe to look like my uncle yeah yeah Dad don't you think it would be nice to maybe look like him?

Bissinger, who divides his time between Philadelphia and the Pacific Northwest, does not spare himself in his work, such as when he wrote a long article for *GQ* on his shopping addiction. The surgically honest piece touched on his purchase of $5,000 pants, $20,000 coats and dozens of boots and gloves. He sets the stage with a critique of Philadelphia fashion:

Fifty-eight-year-old men who live in the nation's capital of fashion dreariness, Philadelphia, where wearing a striped tie with a striped shirt to a cocktail party causes Main Line doyennes to whisper "the horror, the horror" in between the third and fourth martinis and little nibbles on saltines with Velveeta served on silver trays.

Describing his wardrobe, Bissinger writes:

Some of the clothing is men's. Some is women's. I make no distinction. Men's fashion is catching up, with high-end retailers such as Gucci and

Burberry and Versace finally honoring us. But women's fashion is still infinitely more interesting and has an unfair monopoly on feeling sexy, and if the clothing you wear makes you feel the way you want to feel, liberated and alive, then fucking wear it. The opposite, to repress yourself as I did for the first fifty-five years of my life, is the worst price of all to pay. The United States is a country that has raged against enlightenment since 1776; puritanism, the guiding lantern, has cast its withering judgment on anything outside the narrow societal mainstream. Think it's easy to be different in America? Try something as benign as wearing stretch leather leggings or knee-high boots if you are a man.[60]

Gucci, Bissinger reminds the reader, makes up the highest percentage of his collection:

The Gucci brand has always held special power for me, ever since the 1960s, when the Gucci loafer with the horsebit hardware was the rage, and my father, who fancied himself as being anti-status when he secretly loved it, broke down and bought a pair. Followed by my mother's purchase of the famous Jackie O. shoulder bag. As a 13-year-old, I circled the old store on Fifth Avenue several times before getting up the courage to go in and buy a Gucci wallet covered with the insignia.[61]

From fashion, he segues into sexuality: "I never fit the traditional definition of a sexy male straight or gay—tall, ripped, six-packs within six-packs. I wanted the power that sex provides, all eyes wanting to fuck you and you knowing it, and both men's and women's clothing became my venue."

He then begins to wonder about sex and sexuality and where he fits in the complex spectrum:

I did go into the sexual unknown, and the clothing I began to wear routinely gave me the confidence to do it, to transcend the rigid definitions of sexuality and gender, just as I also know there were the requisite stereotypical snickers.

Was I homosexual because so much of what I wore is associated with gays? I did experiment. And while I don't think it is my sexual being, I can tell you that gay men as a group are nicer, smarter, have a shitload more fun than straight whites. Was I veering toward becoming a dominant leather master in the S&M scene, the leather fetish an obvious influence in most of the clothing I purchased and in much of high fashion itself? I did experiment. Was I a closeted or maybe not so closeted transvestite? Tom

Ford makeup is divine; the right foundation and cheek blush and eyeliner and lipstick can do wonders for the pallid complexion. Thigh-high boots add to any wardrobe, although walking on six-inch stilettos for hours is just a bitch and therefore confined to the privacy of my house, seen only by the UPS man, who at this point could not possibly be surprised by anything. But a dress or skirt just doesn't look good on me, and I can't ever do a thing with my hair. The look I was going for was more David Bowie androgynous. It wasn't successful.[62]

Bissinger was saved from his shopping addiction when he signed himself into rehab:

Shortly after I got out of rehab in May of 2013 I put the leather collection into storage. It was well maintained, but it was costing money to keep it home, plus I knew I had to get rid of it as part of my continuing recovery. Through a mutual friend I was put in touch with Matthew Ruiz of LuxeSwap. We corresponded by email. This company is excellent and has done thousands of eBay transactions. He and his wife both used to work in the fashion industry. They asked how much I had. I told them to bring a U-Haul van. It was pretty much filled by the end.

Bissinger says that the experience was cathartic and that it was good "to put a very fucked-up phase of my life to rest." He goes on to explain, "I want to say that the clothing addiction was probably the least of a host of issues that sent me into rehab. There was suicide ideation. I was doing physical harm to myself. I was beginning to play around with drugs such as Percocet."

AT A LECTURE AT THE ATHENAEUM on Philadelphia's Washington Square, the topic was the life of Saint Katharine Drexel, the Catholic saint canonized by Pope John Paul II on October 1, 2000.

The speaker was Cordella Biddle, a direct descendant of Francis Martin Biddle, grandfather of Saint Katharine Drexel and Nicholas Biddle, president of the Second Bank of the United States.

I was looking forward to hearing Biddle talk about her latest book, *Saint Katharine Drexel*, because I had heard that she had inside family stories about what the saint was like as a young woman. The biography is an honest account of Katharine's life, both before and after she gave up the Drexel family fortune and entered religious life.

C. Biddle. *Courtesy of Cordelia Biddle.*

People who give up family fortunes are rare persons, indeed. Most families, in fact, go the opposite route when it comes to inheritances: they squabble, wage war or sue one another over what they think is rightfully theirs. Sometimes the battles get ugly.

Saints exist in most religions, but they are perhaps best understood in Christianity. Protestantism celebrates mainly those saints from the apostolic era, the writers of the Gospels, although in some cases they honor canonized saints up until the time of the Reformation. Protestantism, however, does not "make" new saints. Only Catholicism and Eastern Orthodoxy canonize new saints.

One recent saint of the Catholic Church, aside from Saint Katharine Drexel, is Padre Pio, the Capuchin friar who lived in Pietrelcina, Italy. Padre Pio was clairvoyant in that he could read a person—see into his or her past and even read his or her future. When people came to him for confession, he already knew their sins and what they would confess. He also had the gift of bilocation, being in two places at the same time. When his body was exhumed prior to his canonization, it was found to be incorrupt, meaning that there had been no bodily decay. The long-dead saint looks as though he is sleeping.

This same phenomenon can be found with another Catholic saint, Saint Catherine Laboure of Paris.

Two recent Orthodox saints are Saint John Maximovitch of San Francisco, the Wonderworker, and Saint Elder Paisios, a Greek monk from Mount Athos (a mountain community of monasteries dedicated to the Blessed Virgin). Elder Paisios, like Padre Pio, was clairvoyant; he could read people's sins and see into their pasts or futures. He was a great healer and was known throughout the world as a saint who could bring people back from the brink of death.

My interest in hearing what Cordella Biddle had to say about Katharine Drexel was to get the real scoop about the human Drexel. All too often after saints are canonized, the stories about their lives tend to be unrealistic or "whitewashed." Sickeningly sweet, sanitized saint stories like this are called hagiography, or stories written without the inclusion of human blemish.

Biddle told the audience that when Katharine Drexel was young, she was quite the belle of the ball. Not only was she the best looking among her sisters, but she also got everything she wanted as a teenager. You might say that she had an indulgent father.

Biddle called Katharine "the Paris Hilton of her time," meaning that she was a socialite and a party girl who didn't have a care in the world except when it came to decisions regarding what dress to wear to the next social event.

The future saint also dated boys and at one point turned down an offer of marriage, probably assuming she'd meet someone "better" down the line.

Biddle described what it was like to be at the canonization ceremony in Saint Peter's Square. It was raining very hard that day, she said, and a mass of soaking wet umbrellas covered the square. People were happy despite the rain, although the deluge was so intense that the umbrellas had turned into makeshift drain spouts with water pouring and bouncing off the brims.

And yet, at the precise moment that Katharine Drexel's name was mentioned—there were a number of other people being canonized that day—the rain immediately ceased as if it had been flipped off by a switch. Instantaneously, the sun came out and a rainbow appeared.

She told the audience that she had witnessed a miracle.

In fact, she leaned toward the mic and said the words again: "A miracle!" Miracle is a word that cosmopolitan Athenaeum audiences don't often hear.

The words that one often hears from the Athenaeum stage usually revolve around architecture, art or vague philosophical principles, but they rarely have connections to religion or the life of the soul.

Biddle ended her talk by enumerating on Katharine's wicked sense of humor and how in one of her journals she reduced to mincemeat a wedding she had witnessed in her house as a girl that was attended by then president Ulysses S. Grant. In her journal, Katharine had a lot to say about the bride and her silly, supercilious ways. Biddle told the audience that after reading Katharine's journal entry about the wedding, she sat up in bed one night and realized that she owned the family portrait of the bride about whom Katharine had written.

Biddle is also the author of the Philadelphia-based Victorian-era novels *Deception's Daughter* and *The Conjurer*. These works explore the lives of women in environments of wealth and poverty. In her novel *Beneath the Wind*, Biddle takes a look at imperialism during the Edwardian era. In 1997, she was awarded the SATW Lowell Thomas travel-writing award for her article "Three Perfect Days in Philadelphia."

WHILE "THREE PERFECT DAYS IN PHILADELPHIA" might not touch on the morose subject of where dead journalists go, in the tightfisted, competitive fishbowl world of Philly journalism, once they "go" they are often gone without a trace. Of course, barring the obituary and/or the accompanying news story surrounding the death, after that there's often a great silence. Why should anyone expect more?

Philadelphia Inquirer art critic Edward J. Sozanski died suddenly in his home in Gladwyne, Pennsylvania, in April 2014. Sozanski wrote art criticism for the *Inquirer* for three long decades and was a familiar face among Philly writers and reporters at press events at the Philadelphia Museum of Art (PMA), the Pennsylvania Academy of Art and other institutions. Sozanski was present at many PMA press events, beginning in the early 1990s, when press events for exhibitions were a bigger deal than they are today. In those heady, financially flush days, press events for major PMA exhibitions included a three-course lunch (with wine) in the museum dining room while journalists listened to an array of speakers. At the conclusion of the luncheon, everyone went home with the official exhibition catalogue, which was often an expensive art book costing upward of forty dollars in the museum gift shop.

Philly journalists can be a quirky bunch and do not constitute one big happy family. It's more like a disconnected, dysfunctional, hierarchical family, which is to say that at some press events you have *Philadelphia Inquirer* writers hanging with *Inquirer* or *Philadelphia Daily News* writers, while the scribes for the city's alternative weeklies tend to group together in lower-cast huddles. Occasionally, writers who write for both publications might mix with both groups in a kind of cross-pollination bliss. Magazine writers constitute their own special hierarchy, oblivious of newsprint's "who's who." But press event seating arrangements somehow always seem to change radically whenever a writer from the *New York Times* or a foreign publication visits. Suddenly, the *Inquirer* writers can be seen seated off to the side, as if they wrote for supermarket tabloids. Perhaps the big lesson in this is one of humility.

After Sozanski's death, Stephan Salisbury wrote an *Inquirer* piece about Sozanski in which he stated that the critic was "not distracted by institutional marketing efforts or the city's cultural boosterism." This is no small accomplishment given the pressures to produce good reviews. Salisbury quoted Joseph J. Rishel, PMA's senior curator of European painting before 1900, in which Rishel described Sozanski as being "very thoughtful and very shy." He also stated that Sozanski was "wary of institutional pressure on his critical writing."[63]

Sozanski's piece in the *Philadelphia Inquirer* on the closing of the Barnes Foundation in Merion in preparation for its 2012 move to the Benjamin Franklin Parkway highlights the critic's prescient abilities:

> [The closing of the galleries on] *July 3 won't initiate a simple geographical transition, a brief hiatus in operations as the fabled art collection is trucked eight miles across the city line.*
>
> *The closing of Merion not only marks the end of an era, it also represents a radical transformation in the nature of the institution. In the process, the essential spirit of the place—its genius loci—and a good deal of Albert C. Barnes as well, will be left behind.*
>
> *Barnes Parkway will resemble Barnes Merion in some respects. The 23 galleries are being replicated, so if you were led in blindfolded you wouldn't immediately notice a difference, except perhaps for ambient traffic noise.*
>
> *…But the Replica (or, if you prefer, the Faux Barnes) will be a different institution, a museum with members instead of a school. No more*

Albert C. Barnes. *Courtesy of the Barnes Foundation.*

strolls through the Merion arboretum…and, most important, no more historical context.

Why is this important? Because Barnes Merion is not only one of the world's greatest private art collections, it's also a Gesamtkunstwerk, a comprehensive artwork in itself.

Besides painting, sculpture, and decorative arts galore, Merion also embodies and evokes architecture, horticulture, educational philosophy, American social history, and the personality and taste of the founder.

It can't be relocated organically any more than a giant redwood can be cut off at the knees and stuck in a giant tub on the sidewalk.[64]

Most seasoned city journalists know that at city press events, there are always new waves of what some veterans call kid journalists, first-timers with stationery store–purchased pads and pencils. The majority of these novices will eventually go on to new careers, but there will always be one or two who will stick it out for the long haul. Among veteran Philadelphia authors and journalists is Carol Saline of *Philadelphia* magazine. Saline is a journalist,

Carol Saline. *Courtesy of Larry Robin.*

broadcaster, author and popular public speaker and moderator. She has written eight books, the best known of which comprise the photo essay relationship trilogy she created with photographer Sharon J. Wohlmuth. The first in this series, *Sisters*, spent sixty-three weeks on the *New York Times* bestseller list and sold more than one million copies. It was updated in 2004 in a tenth-anniversary edition. The second book, *Mothers & Daughters*, immediately soared to number one on every national bestseller list; it was followed by *Best Friends*. Saline's solo ventures include *Dr. Snow: How the FBI Nailed an Ivy League Coke King*; *Straight Talk: How to Get Closer to Others by Saying What You Really Mean*; and *A Guide to Good Health*. In 2005, she wrote the essays for the acclaimed photography book *A Day in the Life of the American Woman*.

No book about Philadelphia writers would be complete without the inclusion of literary journalists Bob Ingram and Dan Rottenberg. Ingram is a writer/ journalist/editor whose work has appeared in *Philadelphia* magazine, *Atlantic City* magazine, *South Jersey* magazine, the *Philadelphia Daily News*, *Philadelphia*

Weekly and *Atlantic City Weekly,* among others. In the 1970s, Ingram was the editor of Philadelphia's *Distant Drummer* newspaper, an alternative weekly, although it was referred to in those days as an "underground newspaper." *The Drummer* covered many stories overlooked or ignored by the mainstream press and gave considerable coverage to the merging beat arts scene in literature and politics. In many cases, *The Drummer* was the only place a reader could go for news that the staid mainstream press overlooked or refused to cover. One could also read *The Drummer* to find out what poet Allen Ginsberg did or said when he visited Philadelphia or to read what Philadelphia writers who journeyed to New York's cultural scene were seeing and feeling. The newspaper featured many writers who later went on to become well-known journalists or authors and was considered a must read for anyone interested in the social and cultural upheaval of the 1960s and '70s. Ingram has also co-written, co-produced and narrated a documentary film about the Boardwalk in Wildwood, New Jersey, called *Boardwalk: Greetings from Wildwood By-The-Sea.*

Ingram gives a good overview of those heady countercultural days in an essay about his years at *The Drummer* for the *Broad Street Review:*

Bob Ingram. *Courtesy of Bob Ingram.*

Victor Bockris and Andrew Wylie were two of my favorites. Victor was a skinny little Brit, a Penn graduate, who's long been a fixture on the offbeat New York literary scene, and Andrew, cum laude at Harvard, became the enfant terrible of big-time literary agents—known tellingly as "the Jackal"—with clients who range from the late Elmore "Dutch" Leonard to Salman Rushdie. He started the Wylie Agency in 1980, and they don't get any bigger.

Strangely, I never met Andrew, who remained in the Big Apple while Victor schlepped down to provincial Philly to deliver their loopy joint interviews with the likes of Muhammad Ali, Salvador Dalí, and Allen Ginsberg. I think I paid them $10 or $15 a pop. They didn't care. They were making their bones.

One time when Victor was in town, our mutual friend, the late poet Otis Brown—O.B., his bad self—brought him over to my apartment at Third and Bainbridge. We smoked some fine weed and then my girlfriend said she had to go out and said good-bye to everybody and split. Trouble was, she locked the door from the outside and took the only key with her and the only way to unlock that door was with that key. There were no latches or anything on the inside, so we were effectively locked in.

Now Victor Bockris, unlike me and O.B., didn't smoke much, and the weed really got hold of him and he told me he had to go out and get some fresh air. Well, when I told him about us being locked in, he went pale and I thought he was going to swoon dead away. So we got him to a comfy chair and, him being a Brit, I got him a nice mug of tea and, luckily, my girlfriend wasn't gone long. I wonder if Victor remembers that?

…Muhammad Ali was at his zenith then, the most famous and popular figure in the world. He was up at his training camp in Deer Lake in the Pennsylvania Poconos, when up show Bockris-Wylie wanting to interview him, but not as a boxer—as a poet! And Ali went for it like it was an opportunity from Allah Himself. Here was the Greatest, the self-proclaimed King of the World, and here were these two twerps in Brooks Brothers suits and weird accents who thought it would be interesting to interview Ali as a serious-ass poet. Whooee! He kept them up there for about a week, rapping and joking and having serious poetry talks and everybody loved it.[65]

Prolific editor and writer Dan Rottenberg is the author of ten books, including *Death of a Gunfighter: The Quest for Jack Slade, the West's Most Elusive*

Dan Rottenberg. *Courtesy of Dan Rottenberg.*

Legend (2008); *Main Line Wasp* (1990), the memoirs of iconic Philly civic leader W. Thacher Longstreth; *Finding Our Fathers: A Guidebook to Jewish Genealogy*; and *The Outsider: Albert M. Greenfield and the Fall of the Protestant Establishment.* He is the former executive editor of *Philadelphia* magazine and managing editor of the *Chicago Journalism Review* and has never been one to run from controversy. As former chief editor of the *Welcomat* (now the *Philadelphia Weekly*), Rottenberg stood his ground when challenged by militant ideologues in an age when challenging extreme leftist orthodoxies put one on editorial "no fly" lists. Rottenberg lives in Philadelphia with his wife, a piano teacher, while his two grown daughters make their home in New York City. Rottenberg told the *University of Pennsylvania Gazette*:

My grandfather, Marc, became a disciple of Mordecai Kaplan, founder of Reconstructionism, the notion that Judaism is not so much a religion as a civilization that has constantly been "reconstructed." My relatives taught me that great ideas do not begin as a minority of one. They often occur simultaneously to many people in isolation, but the ideas perish unless a community connects such people.

Rottenberg's book *Death of a Gunfighter* documents the writer's journey to Colorado to uncover information about Jack Slade (1831–64), an Old West gunfighter as portrayed by Mark Twain in *Roughing It*. Slade was a man of mystery because, despite a notorious reputation for drunkenness and gun violence as a wagonmaster, an Overland Mail division superintendent, he kept the mail and the stagecoaches in operation. Slade's drunkenness brought him to a tragic end: he was hanged by a group of Montana vigilantes.

Rottenberg writes:

If you cross the Union Pacific tracks and the South Platte River from Julesburg and head west along the River Road, you will soon find yourself alone. No motorist stumbles accidentally upon this gravel strip, which extends only some 10 miles and leads nowhere. Nor will you encounter much traffic anywhere else in this remote northeast corner of Colorado: Sedgwick County contains fewer than 2,800 inhabitants.

He goes on to say that he has come to this desolate road because he is on a historical detective quest:

My quarry has been dead for nearly a century and a half, but even in death he has eluded a long line of distinguished authors and Western devotees, just as in life he eluded his friends and foes alike—everyone, in fact, but his worst enemy: himself. I have pursued his trail for half a century on a mission to sift the truth of my character's life from his legend. Where Mark Twain, Zane Grey, and the late Montana Chief Justice Llewellyn Link Callaway have tried and failed, I am determined to succeed.[66]

In *The Outsider: Albert M. Greenfield and the Fall of the Protestant Establishment*, Rottenberg reminds readers that "for centuries before Albert M. Greenfield was born, many gentiles and even some Jews themselves believed that the descendents of Abraham, Issac and Jacob possessed some sort of cultural if not genetic gift for finance and commerce." History, however, offers a different slant, and Rottenberg is quick to add that this wasn't always the case:

> *With a few exceptions (like King Solomon, the first great Jewish exporter), the Hebrews of ancient Israel were largely farmers, craftsmen, and warriors who for the most part lacked commercial acumen. The Torah, for all its complex regulations concerning the conduct of everyday life, said little about the conduct of business, most likely because commerce played such a minor role among the Jews of antiquity.[67]*

PHILADELPHIA IS A POPULAR LECTURE destination for international writers wishing to promote new books. The Central Branch of the city's Free Library system has become a major venue for many well-known names. One writer and novelist with a significant Philadelphia connection was Susan Sontag, who first lectured in the city in the spring of 1967 after the publication of her seminal book of essays, *Against Interpretation*. *Against Interpretation* was then the talk of the nation, while Sontag's second volume of essays, *Styles of Radical Will*, would be published shortly thereafter. The first Sontag volume included the famous essay on camp. The Vietnam War, then in full swing, was also beginning to season Sontag's political and antiwar views. She was, as they say, hot property.

Dubbed "the Dark Lady of American Letters" because of her good looks and her reputation as a brainy wunderkind—"the Natalie Wood of the U.S. Avant-garde," as *Contemporary Biography* declared—many saw her as the successor of novelist/essayist Mary McCarthy. "Dark Lady" or not, at the Free Library podium in 1967 she certainly presented an artful persona. Walking onstage in an opera cape, she had the habit of flipping her great mane of hair off her forehead while taking periodic tokes from a long cigarette holder. Those personal touches suggested the decadence of Oscar Wilde, who had visited and fascinated the city almost one hundred years earlier, or the poetry of Baudelaire.

Romantic, perverse literary glamour had come to Philadelphia. This was a far cry from the matronly gloved and hated Pearl S. Buck.

Nancy Kates's film, *Regarding Susan Sontag*, had its Philadelphia premier at the Jewish Museum. The effervescent Kates described meeting Sontag years earlier at a Meet Susan Sontag Night on the campus of the University of Chicago. Kates, who had been struggling with a paper on Jackson Pollack, found the artistic answers she was looking for in Sontag's essays in *Against*

Interpretation, but when she went to tell Sontag about her euphonious discovery, she says that the diva looked at her "with utter disdain," as if she were thinking, "I have better things to work on than helping a hapless undergrad."

When I asked Kates about her impressions of Sontag, she described her as "condescending, imperialistic and difficult" and says she doubts whether Sontag would even approve of her film. Sontag, in fact, had gone to extreme lengths to stop publication of a 2000 unauthorized biography, *Susan Sontag: The Making of an Icon* by Carl Rollyson and Lisa Paddock. (The book was subsequently published and became a bestseller). Kates decided to do the film despite Sontag's rebuff and despite the fact that more than one person asked her if she had taken on the project out of a spirit of revenge. The question shocked her. "I'd have to be pretty screwed up to want revenge for something that happened twenty or twenty-five years ago," she said.

In the 1980s, when the *Philadelphia Inquirer* published a short piece announcing that Sontag was teaching a graduate seminar at Temple University, I requested an interview.

Sontag called back that very afternoon. Luckily, I already had a few questions scribbled on a notepad in case the unexpected happened. I knew that every word I uttered would filter through the Sontag Analysis Machine and that she'd be quick with a verdict: was I worthy to interview her?

Not only was the "Natalie Wood of American Literature" unusually friendly, but she also agreed to get in touch when she could schedule a meeting.

Some weeks passed and I heard nothing, but then, in the mail, a letter (dated May 4, 1986) arrived from Farrar, Straus & Giroux: "Forgive me for not answering your letter sooner. The time I have in Philadelphia was very compressed and every minute of it each week was accounted for, so in the end I could not find time to do the interview you requested." She closed with a pleasant personal note, "I wish you every success with your writing."

In the years that followed, I made it a point to go up to her after her lectures, whether at the University of Pennsylvania (where I took one of her theater seminars), at the Free Library or at her big Marianne Moore talk at Friends Select School, sponsored by the Rosenbach Museum and Library.

As for the snub that Nancy Kates experienced from Sontag in Chicago, I felt a similar jab after her Free Library talk on staging Samuel Beckett's *Waiting for Godot* in Bosnia.

I had asked her a personal question about a Harvard professor acquaintance of hers from the 1970s who was once also a friend of mine and who apparently had given her a lift in his convertible MG from Provincetown to Boston.

While retelling the Provincetown story, I could see something shift in her eyes.

"My God," she said, squaring her eyes with mine, "that was a long time ago." I should have fled when I noticed the corners of her mouth turn down, but I stayed put until she shut me down by turning her back to me and focusing on a young woman from Bosnia sitting near her.

My last meetings with Sontag before her death in 2004 included an event sponsored by the Rosenbach Museum in which she spoke on photography and the poetry of Marianne Moore. Once again, we had an opportunity to chat, albeit on the run, as she was headed out to dinner with the Rosenbach brass.

"Philadelphia is so weird," she said, laughing. "What other American city would put a clothespin in the middle of downtown?"

Did she say "weird?" Was this the same woman who praised the novels of William S. Burroughs and who found much to like in the anti-novels of the French avant-garde?

The last encounter was at a two-day event at the Kelly Writer's House, where I'd gone on the second day to hear her read from her work and participate in a Q&A. Arriving late for the pre-lecture breakfast, I joined the crowd around the buffet table and collided with a woman in a dark sweater who was going for the same cream cheese dip I was aiming for.

I was surprised when I discovered that the woman was none other than Sontag herself.

"Oh…hello there," she said before being ushered away by Kelly Writers House brass for her seat behind the table lectern.

During the lecture, I asked her how she weathered the storm caused by her essay on September 11 in the *New Yorker*.

The essay was written in fifteen minutes, she said, and she didn't think it controversial at all when she sent it off. After the essay's publication, the vehemence with which she was attacked was unlike anything she'd experienced to date. Even her anti–Vietnam War stance did not attract the same kind of hatred and viciousness.

True to form, Sontag turned a stoic's eye to the anger and death threats.

As Kates told me, "She did pretend that she was Athena springing from the head of Zeus."

POETDELPHIA

Philadelphia is sometimes called "Poetdelphia" because it's easy to find a poet on every street corner. Philadelphia also boasts many city-based poetry magazines and zines like the *American Poetry Review*, the *Painted Bride Quarterly*, the *Philadelphia Poets Journal* and the *New Purlieu Review*. Every year in April (or National Poetry Month), Larry Robin of Moonstone (once part of the now-defunct Robin's Bookstore) hosts Poetry Ink, in which hundreds of poets sign up for an opportunity to read their work on stage for three or four minutes. Poetry Ink is an all-day event. It's a chance for the city's poets to come together and network. The huge range of poets in Philadelphia includes:

Good lady poets sometimes come to Moonstone dressed like Emily Dickinson; there are "come to Jesus" poets who list the things that Jesus has done for them lately; girlfriend-boyfriend poets who write about their love for each other; and female poets (dressed in black) who write about how they got even with cruel ex-boyfriends, while spurned boyfriend poets write about their "Medusa ex-girlfriends" who are "still on the loose." There are also purely sexual poets who go right to the G-spot with words and images meant to shock; jazz poets who try to sound like Ella Fitzgerald; first-time poets who blush and stutter and are afraid to make eye contact with the audience; black activist poets who remind us of the evils of slavery; academic poets who do their best to ape Virgil's *The Aeneid* or the lyric poetry of Quintus Horatuis Flaccus (Horace) but, more often than not, just make the audience yawn; and slam poets who combine their words with body

Above: The Philadelphia skyline at night. *Courtesy of Robert Gordon.*

Left: Herschel Baron. *Courtesy of Larry Robin.*

motions—a wiggle or twerk here, a palsy arm spasm there—before they end it all with throwback "operatic" head motions. There are also retro, San Francisco-style, goatee-sporting beat poets who scream louder than they should as the cocked fedora on their heads fall to the floor; the mom-with-grown-children poets from Cherry Hill who like to talk about their rabbis; or the angry ex-Catholic poets with stories of priests and nuns. There are poets who take fifteen minutes to explain the poem they are about to read or who take twenty-five minutes to read a series of poems after promising to be brief. There are poets who approach the podium with a portfolio of notes. Some of these poets are champions at self-promotion and will spend five minutes filling you in on how to buy their discounted books on Amazon. Finally, there are poets who breathe heavily into the microphone, the listen-to-my-breathing poets who should really have been singers or dancers.

There are very good poets at Moonstone, which makes Poetry Ink worth the effort.

Sonia Sanchez, the city's first poet laureate (Philadelphia's current poet laureate is Frank Sherlock), had an exceptional ability to work with mainstream audiences through the city's Mural Arts Project. "The black artist is dangerous," Sanchez has written. "Black art controls the 'Negro's' reality, negates negative influences, and creates positive images."[68] Born in Alabama in 1934 as Wilsonia Benita Driver, she graduated from New York's Hunter College after moving to Harlem as a young girl and then studied for a while at New York University under Louise Bogan. She married Albert Sanchez but kept his surname after her divorce and remarriage to poet Etheridge Knight. Well known as an activist for racial equality, Sanchez began her years as a teacher at San Francisco State in 1965 and joined the Nation of Islam in 1972 because of then burgeoning views on black separatism, but she left the organization in 1975 due to

Sonia Sanchez. *Courtesy of Larry Robin.*

121

that group's views on women's rights. Her more than twelve published poetry volumes include *Morning Haiku* (2010) and *Does Your House Have Lions?* (1995).

In 2011, the seventy-seven-year-old poet, teacher and activist in Philadelphia was named the city's first poet laureate by Mayor Michael Nutter in a ceremony at city hall. Since that time, she has appeared in many poetry readings throughout the city, along with other local poets who have begun to establish national reputations, like Philadelphia's CAConrad, who writes that his childhood consisted of "selling cut flowers along the highway for his mother and helping her shoplift."[69] Conrad continues to stun audiences with his *Deviant Propulsion* word missiles (e.g., "It's True I Tell Ya My Father Is a 50 cent Party Balloon"). The award-winning poet is the author of many books and chapbooks, including *The Frank Poems*, *Advanced Elvis Course* and *(end-begin w/chants)*, a collaboration with Philadelphia's current poet laureate, Frank Sherlock. Attending a CAConrad reading can be an unforgettable experience. Part stand-up comic, slam theater experience, Conrad dazzles with oversized rhinestone glasses, feathers or even bathtub recitations.

With poem titles like "I Still Have Keys to the Apartment," "Bran Muffins Have Nothing to Do With It! So There!" and "Leaving the Only Bed in

Jim Cory, Janet Mason, and C.A. Conrad are Insight to Riot!

The Scoop
Presents
Insight To Riot
A Philadelphia based Poetry Troupe
Performance date:
April 16th, 1994
Performance Times:
8:30 PM & 10:30 PM
Tickets available
at The Scoop
5 South 8th Street
Allentown PA
(215) 434-9766
Don't Miss It!

Poets CAConrad, Jim Cory and Janet Mason. *Courtesy of Jim Cory.*

America That Keeps Me Satisfied," Conrad's irreverent style might not go over at the city's Union League, but his cult following is symbolic of poetry's status in the city. The "new-style" Philadelphia poet is often cantankerously unique and sports some sort of physical signature like a big hat, a monocle or several scarves. These styles have given poetry an urban mystique.

The poetic signature look is an apt description that can be applied to poet Lamont Steptoe, who grew up in Pittsburgh and found his wings as a poet while serving in the Republic of South Vietnam from 1969 to 1970 as a scout dog handler, meaning someone whose job it was to walk point element for combat patrols. Assigned to the Twenty-fifth Infantry at Cu Chi, the accomplished poet, photographer and founder of Whirlwind Press has published many volumes of poetry, including *Crimson River* and *American Morning/Mourning*. Steptoe could be a future Philadelphia poet laureate, despite his antiwar polemic. For years, Steptoe could be seen walking around town in army fatigues, heavy back gear, a large Miraculous Medal and other talismans as if the gritty streets of the city were the jungles of Indo-China.

In "Toxic Waste," Steptoe writes:

> *'Nam*
> *was a radioactive war*
> *No nuclear bombs*
> *were dropped*
> *Years later*
> *Some GIs put guns*
> *to temple*
> *or aimed at others*
> *Some*
> *rotted away internally*
> *dying in orange light*

In "Returning the Missing," the remains of soldiers come home from war:

> *Boxes*
> *smaller than bodies*
> *returning the missing home*
> *Dog tags*
> *and wood*
> *fragments of bone*
> *All that's left*

Fifth Annual Black Writers Conference. *Courtesy of Larry Robin.*

of Johnny
Jimmy
Jose
Leroy
Willie
or Jake
All that's left
of history
impassioned mystery
sundown of mistake

Whenever a city committee assembles to select a poet laureate, the personal becomes political. Would a vegetarian, Asian, female poet laureate with a penchant for Marxism be a safer bet than, say, a latter-day Paul Goodman ("He was a beautiful mechanic / till his wife cut him down to size")? If Philly poet Alexandra Grilikhes were alive today, would her various poems to female lovers in books like *The Reveries, The Blue Scar, On Women Artists* and *Isabel Rawsthorne Standing in a Street in Soho*

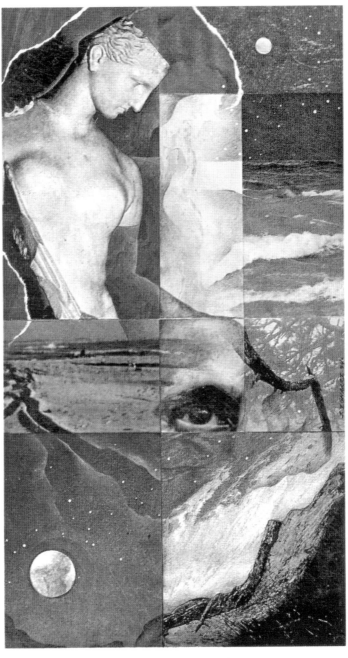

THE REVERIES

POEMS /   ALEXANDRA GRILIKHES

be deemed too risqué? On the other hand, would a waspish W.H. Auden or a T.S. Eliot type be dismissed as too "white bread," too Anglo-Catholic or formalist? Or what about that "safe mom poet" with three names who likes to write about Longwood Gardens, the Devon Horse Show or the Liberty Bell? While a poet like this wouldn't upset a conventional Union League audience, what would happen if, overnight, this same safe mom poet ended up sounding like Sylvia Plath?

Ideally, a poet laureate should appeal to a great many people, which means that his or her body of work should not be too classical, angry, political, obtuse, obscure, dense, out there or even slam-theatrical. In Poetdelphia, this may be a hard bill to fill, although one immediately thinks of Daisy Fried, a Philadelphia poet whose work has been praised by novelist Joyce Carol Oates, who described it as "fluid and quicksilver as life seen close up." Oates goes on to say, "Here is an original voice: provocative, poignant, and often very funny."[70] Fried is the author of three books of poetry, including *My Brother Is Getting Arrested Again*.

DEFINITELY NOT IN THE "GETTING ARRESTED" category is the Reverend John P. McNamee, pastor emeritus of Saint Malachy Church in North Philadelphia, who was ordained a priest by John Cardinal O'Hara in 1959. Father McNamee, who has spent most of his priesthood serving the poor and disadvantaged, is credited with bringing Dorothy Day's Catholic Worker movement to Philadelphia. An award-winning poet, his books *Clay Vessels* and *Endurance—The Rhythm of Faith* have been popular spiritual bestsellers. His autobiography, *Diary of a City Priest*, won the Catholic Press Association Book Award and was made into a movie for television starring actor David Morse in 2001. An international speaker, Father McNamee received a doctor of humanities honorary degree from Villanova University in 2001. In 2006, he published *Donegal Suite*, a collection of contemplative and mystical poems that derives from a summer of solitude he spent in Northern Ireland. The second half of the book concentrates more on the pathos of daily life in Philadelphia.

In the poem "Gweedore" from *Donegal Suite*, McNamee confesses:

> *What I know is that one wild afternoon on*
> *the Giant's Causeway in County Antrim*
> *wind and salt-spray, the smell of kelp and a*
> *walk on wet lichen-covered basalt columns*
> *was home as never elsewhere am I home*

Poets Essex Hemphill and Bob Small. *Courtesy Lamont Steptoe.*

> *My long-dead father's place not fifty*
> *kilometers south. He, Scots and Irish, and*
> *if sight could piece the horizontal rain, there*
> *the Mull of Kintyre north across the water.*
> *Tousled and wet, I returned to an inn*
> *back from the headland where the smell*
> *of tobacco on damp wool mixed with*
> *the odors brought from their farms by*
> *old men gathered with pints around a fireplace.*
> *A home I was visiting for the first time.*

McNamee's poem "Easter" evokes his admiration for the Trappist monk peace activist writer Thomas Merton:

> *Early Thomas Merton made us all*
> *alter ego monks   eager visitors*
> *heavy-eyed at vigils*
> *singing in morning with Trappists*
> *behind Psalters so huge that*
> *page turning was a two-man job.*

WHILE THE MYSTICAL POEMS of a priest might not be ideal to represent the city of Philadelphia, a secular mystic poet like Leonard Gontarek, might be a good choice. Gontarek is a contributing editor of the Philadelphia-founded and based *American Poetry Review*, the author of five books of poems, including *St. Genevieve Watching Over Paris, Van Morrison Can't Find His Feet* and *Zen for Beginners*. Gontarek is also the recipient of five Pushcart Prize nominations, and his poetry workshops have become legendary in the city. Gontarek's biting cerebral writing style avoids the political obviousness of a Conrad or a Steptoe. Like Oklahoma City–born poet Jim Cory, author of a number of books and chapbooks and editor of the 1997 Black Sparrow Press edition of James Broughton's poems, *Packing Up For Paradise*, Gontarek's Wallace Stevens insurance salesman persona means that neither he nor Cory would be "recognized" as poets in the street, at least if one is going by the "uniform" of younger urban poets, which tends toward affectation, such as the arrangement of neck scarves. This style can range from the minimalist placement of one scarf to the piling on of two or three so that one thinks of café habitués in Paris or of certain Middle Eastern revolutionaries. While the poetic uniform is usually relegated to the young—consider prose writer George Lippard's flamboyant dress—other poets seem happier to blend with the scenery in much the same way that Walt Whitman, who dressed as if he were a farmer, blended in with his Camden townsfolk.

Jim Cory's most recent chapbook is *No Brainer Variations* (Rain Mountain Press, 2011). Cory is also the recipient of fellowships from the Pennsylvania Arts Council, Yaddo and the MacDowell Colony. His poems have appeared in a number of publications, including *Apiary, Bedfellows, Whirlwind* and *Skidrow Penthouse*.

He believes that poetry can be different things to different people at different times, and he told me that when he was twelve, he stumbled on *The Mentor Book of Major American Poets* on the paperback rack at the Stamford Museum and Nature Center (in Connecticut):

> *It was sacred text. It explained everything. I still have it. Five years later, it was all about the Beats and Bohemian rebellion. Fast-forward ten years and a lot of what I was writing was gay poetry. In my sixties, I write in different modes to satisfy different ends. Short poems appeal because of the challenge of getting something complicated into seven lines, cut-ups and collage because they're fun and with any luck can be fun for the reader too.*

PAUL ROBESON IN WORDS

PETE SEEGER as himself

America's wandering minstral, composer of songs we sang, and sing today, and a vital part of the history of artists who fought for freedom and justice, he was a close friend to Paul Robeson. Tonight he brings his memories and his talents to this memorial.

EARL ROBINSON as himself & Larry Brown

A living monument to America's great music, and a fearless advocate of fairness to all men, his "Ballad for Americans" broadcast on CBS radio with Paul Robeson, under Andre Kostalonitz, gave hope and spirit to troubled America.

JOHN ANTHONY as Paul Robeson

John made his debut at the Metropolitan Opera in 1985 in Porgy and Bess, sang the world premiere of Leonard Bernstein's Mass at the Kennedy Center and has sung with the Pittsburgh Symphony, Cleveland Symphony and many others. He has appeared on Broadway in Hello Dolly, Jimmy, Oklahoma and Sweet Charity, plus TV & films.

Also Featuring
DAVE SAWYER • LUCY MURHY • JUDY GORMAN • CHRIS OWENS

Executive Producer	JOYCE BROWN
Producer & Director	MARTI ROGERS
Production and Script	LARRY RUBIN
Slide Production	TOM LEVY
Slide Editing	MARTI ROGERS
Lighting	STACY SMITH
Sound & Recording	Kennedy Studios, DAVID KENNEDY

A MOONSTONE Inc. & SWORDS INTO PLOUGHSHARES PRESENTATION
With special thanks to the Board of Education, City of Philadelphia
and Dr. Davis Martin, Principal, University City High School

Interpreted for the
hearing impaired
by SUSAN LEVITON

"Paul Robeson in Words." *Courtesy of Larry Robin.*

Cory also believes that it is important for poets to take poetry—"not their poetry but poetry in the broad sense—more seriously than they take themselves."

The one book he would salvage if books were about to disappear would be *The Random House Book of Twentieth Century French Poetry*. He says

Poets Lamont Steptoe, Jim Cory, Sonia Sanchez, Margaret Randall and Amrita David. *Courtesy of Larry Robin.*

he doesn't know how he came across the book or even who recommended it, but it was his constant literary companion twenty-five years ago, and reading it changed how he wrote because it encouraged rule-breaking, "such as the use of non-sequiturs, elimination of conjunctions, ability to shape the poem on the page in ways that reflect its tone or spirit."

In his poem "1923–2001," Cory writes:

> *boxes, boxes, boxes, mother said*
> *sitting in the living room*
> *of her senior citizen condo*
>
> *on moving day*
> *look at all these*
> *goddamned boxes*
>
> *she shook her head*
> *& lit*
> *another cigarette*

the next time I move
they'll be one box
& I'll be in it

A thoroughly urbane poet, in "5 x 25," Cory announces:

No I don't have change let alone to spare
Unsparing on days I know it'll take
8 or 9 lifetimes
to thaw the iceberg
this city's grown inside me

or,

Sarah liked to give people things
& call years later demanding them back
hon, is that road map of Mongolia still in your apartment?
I need my spiderweb cloud key please…
Dropping by to retrieve that trapeze act, okay?

Or even…

Phil + Clare '76 etched in cement
There on American Street
Where has time flung these
Young lovers & their misbegotten century
Alive? Married? Mummies in some museum?

PHILADELPHIA'S MOST FAMOUS MODERN POET, who almost always wore a suit and tie, was the 1973–74 poet laureate of the United States, Daniel Hoffman. Hoffman's poetry is almost always just a little sad, but it is also noted for its joy in the small things of life. As he once told an interviewer, "Even when a poet writes about something negative the fact that he puts it into a form controls it, makes it positive." The author of more than twenty-five books moved to Philadelphia in 1948 with his wife, poet Elizabeth MacFarland. At this time, Philadelphia was on the verge of a rebirth, just a few years before architect Vincent Kling and city planner Edmund Bacon would change the face of downtown. It was also the era of Mayor Richardson Dilworth, the first Democratic mayor after decades of "corrupt and contented" Republican politics. Change was in the air, and Hoffman, feeling the pulse, felt no leftover homesickness for New York City, which he once labeled "a city that cannibalizes its own past."

At the time of his arrival in Philadelphia, McFarland was poetry editor of the *Ladies' Home Journal* in the city's Washington Square neighborhood, once a major publishing hub. Hoffman, who in school had been a classmate of poet Allen Ginsberg, went on to teach English and poetry at the University of Pennsylvania. By all accounts, he became a good teacher yet admitted that he'd be the first to castigate a student if he heard that the student did not read poetry by other poets because of the fear of influence. Blunt to a fault, Hoffman said that he wouldn't want students like this in his class, even though he expressed sensitivity toward the pitfalls of being a seventeen-year-old beginning poet, for whom all poetry generally means "my love affair." Young poets of this caliber, Hoffman explains, all write "the same verbal spaghetti without any control or form," all the more reason to make them "read good poetry."[71] One teaching method he used to cure the "my love affair" view of poetry was to copy out police reports and have the students choose one and then write a poem about why the culprit was arrested. This exercise was important, he says, to get the students "out of themselves."

Henry Winkler and Larry Robin. *Courtesy of Larry Robin.*

Larry Robin. *Courtesy of Larry Robin.*

Born in 1923, Hoffman's books include *The Whole Nine Yards: Longer Poems*; *Makes You Stop and Think: Sonnets*; and *Brotherly Love*, a National Book Award winner. He's the author of seven volumes of criticism and *Zones of the Interior: A Memoir, 1942–1947*. Perhaps Hoffman's best-known prose work is *Poe Poe Poe Poe Poe Poe Poe*, a critical and sometimes humorous study of Poe's works. When the widely anthologized Hoffman was asked what he thought of modern and postmodern poetry, he replied that in the mansion of poetry, "there are many rooms; there's different kinds of excellence," and the poet must "do what you can your own way." Always a teacher at heart, when asked if he thought that modern confessional poetry was self-indulgent, he explained that confessional poetry came about as a "rebellion against the impersonal, metaphysical, intellectualized complex lyricism that Eliot both by precept and example had established." Two examples of powerful confessional poetry, he says, are the work of Sylvia Path and Robert Lowell's powerful masterpiece, "Life Studies." As for confessional poetry in general, he attributes that revolution to the work of W.D. Snodgrass (1928–2009) in that poet's Pulitzer Prize–winning book, *Heart's Needle*.[72] Hoffman was a member of Philadelphia's Franklin Inn for many years. He died on March 30, 2013, in Haverford, Pennsylvania.

French poet Arthur Rimbaud's line "You must change your life" set the tone for future poets, including Philadelphia's Daniel Abdal-Hayy Moore. Born in 1940 in Oakland, California, Moore's first book of poems, *Dawn Visions*, was published in 1964 by Lawrence Ferlinghetti of City Lights Books. This was the beat generation era, when Allen Ginsberg's *Howl*, also published by City Lights, was changing the poetic landscape. In 1972, Moore followed up with another City Lights volume, *Burnt Heart/Ode to the War Dead*, about the human carnage in Vietnam. In the late 1960s, he founded and directed the Floating Lotus Magic Opera Company in Berkeley, California, and later presented two major productions, *The Walls Are Running Blood* and *Bliss Apocalypse*. The world was changing, and for some this meant a reinvention of the self. For Moore—who was then a self-described Zen Buddhist whose normal routine was to get up early every morning, "sit zazen, smoke a joint, do half an hour of yoga, then read the Mathnawi of Rumi, the long mystical poem of that great Persian Sufi of the thirteenth century"—life was about to change.[73]

He met the man who was to be his spiritual guide, Shaykh Muhammad ibn al-Habib. "The man looked like an eccentric Englishman," Moore writes.

> *He too had only recently come out of the English version of the Hippie Wave. He was older, refined in his manners, spectacularly witty and intellectual, but of that kind prevalent then who had hobnobbed with the Beatles and knew the Tantric Art collection of Brian Jones firsthand. He had been on all the classic drug quests—peyote in the Yucatan, mescaline with Laura Huxley—but with the kif quest in Morocco he had stumbled on Islam, and then the Sufis, and the game was up. A profound change had taken place in his life that went far beyond the psychedelic experience.*[74]

Moore converted to Sufi Islam in 1970, riding a wave of spiritual self-transformation that affected other writers and poets in the Bay area, most notably Eugene Rose (Seraphim Rose), an atheist and Marxist whose devotion to Nietzsche nearly drove him mad before he read the writings of the Christian Desert Fathers. Rose, who would go on to become an Orthodox priest and co-founder of Holy Trinity monastery near Redding, California, is now considered by many to be a future saint of the Russian Orthodox Church. As for Moore, his spiritual transformation inspired him to travel to Morocco, Spain, Algeria and Nigeria and finally back to California, where he would publish *The Desert Is the Only Way Out*.

In many ways, Philadelphia would prove to be Moore's desert, although he did not become a Philadelphian until 1990. Before that date, he lived for a while in Boston's North End, where he remembers meeting poet John Weiners, the shy Irish Catholic poet to whom Allen Ginsberg once referred as "a pure poet" and who was really the Walt Whitman of New England.

Moore told me that he met John Weiners in 1965 when Weiners worked at Filene's Basement in Boston:

> *Weiners was in a "circle" of poets with David Rattray, Steve Jolas, etc., and we meet a few times at a poetry afternoon at Jola's place…I walked with John and Denise Levertov to the train station where John took a train back home, and probably to be institutionalized for a while…I didn't know him well, but he came to our apartment in the North End a few times and said little, wrote a poem once, and left…Once he came when we had a little room with Xmas lights on the ceiling, and he went in there, lay down, and we forgot he was there until an hour later he appeared in our little kitchen and left…He was a wraithlike soul…Died alone in the snow after a New Years party…on his way home.*

The Milton, Massachusetts born Weiners, who studied at Black Mountain College with Robert Creely and Robert Duncan, was part of the beat poetry renaissance in San Francisco but always called himself a Boston poet. Bruce Chatwin, in a letter to his wife, Elizabeth, sometime in 1972, writes of San Francisco at that time as being "utterly light-weight and sugary with no sense of purpose or depth. The people are overcome with an incurable frivolity whenever they set foot in it. This doesn't mean that one couldn't live here. In fact I think one could easily, preferably with something equally frivolous to do." Chatwin was equally unimpressed with Duncan. He confides to Elizabeth:

> *We went one night to the grand San Francisco poet Robert Duncan who is famous with the young for his grandiloquent and skillful outburst on the Vietnam War. I on the other hand thought him one of the most unpleasant people I have ever met, with a waxen witch-like face, hair tied in a pigtail and a pair of ludicrous white sideburns. He gassed on and on in a flat monotone and it was impossible to decide if the tone was hysterical or dead pan.*

Boston, an elder sister city to Philadelphia with many historic similarities, was dear to Weiners:

> *Boston, sooty in memory, alive with a*
> *thousand murky dreams of adolescence*

135

still calls to youth; the wide streets, chimney tops over
Charles River's broad sweep to seahood buoy;
    the harbor
With dreams, too…

Slumbering city, what makes men think you sleep,
but breathe, what chants or paeans needed
    at this end, except
you stand as first town, first bank of hopes,
    first envisioned
paradise…

While living in Philadelphia, Moore published *The Ramadan Sonnets* (Jusoor/City Lights) and, in 2002, *The Blind Beekeeper* (Jusoor/Syracuse University Press). San Francisco poet, playwright and novelist Michael McClure has written that Moore's poems are like Frank O'Hara's, where "there are no boundaries or limits to possible subject matter" and where "imagination runs rampant and it glides."

In his poem "Great Cruelty and Heartlessness," Moore writes:

We're living in a time of great cruelty and heartlessness
where instead of a sun they're throwing up
anvils
Instead of sunlight there's the sound of
hammers beating
Instead of walking there's kicking
Instead of thinking there's talking
It's almost as if there've never been times like
these before
Even shadows thrown by cartwheels on dirt roads
resemble the grimaces of armies as they
slide across rocks
In the palaces of power clocks go off but no one
wakes
Decisions are made by pouring acid down drains
or waiting for nightfall in a room lit by
neon tubes
If anyone speaks all eyes are upon them
I saw a sparrow fly over a fence

An ant stop and not go on
But laughter has turned to pebbles
falling on zinc
And children have been torn from their futures

Moore is not a poet of empty things and ideas but aspects of the spiritual, as the divine seems to invade every word he writes. He was viewed as legendary in the California of the 1960s, in part because he was able to be "spiritual" without losing his sense of humor. He is the spiritual poet with a comedic wink.

Moore works with Larry Robin at Philadelphia's Moonstone Arts Center, where he helps coordinate Moonstone's annual Poetry Ink readings of 100 Poets. He has also worked as poetry editor for *Seasons Journal*, *Islamica* magazine, a 2010 translation by Munir Akash of *State of Siege* by Mahmoud Darwish (Syracuse University Press) and *The Prayer of the Oppressed* by Imam Muhammad Nasir al-Dar'i. In 2011, 2012 and 2014, he was awarded the Nazim Hikmet Prize for Poetry, and in 2013, he won an American Book Award.

In this age of ongoing dialogue among Muslims, Christians and Jews, the sacred person known as the Virgin Mary is mentioned some thirty-four times in the Koran. The sacred person concept is not lost on Moore, who writes in "Five Short Meditations on the Virgin Mary":

I saw Mary board a bus at Broad and State
her head covered and her face radiant
small and held within herself
careful and preoccupied
a heaven seeming to be wrapped around her
her cheeks red her lips dry her eyes lowered
interior moisture her preferred cloister
the bus passengers sudden ghosts before her
her shoes small and tattered
her hands carrying a book
If any had spoken to her she might have become lost
If she had spoken to anyone
they might have become saved

IF THE POET ELEANOR WILNER could be saved from anything, it would be a sore throat. "I have the throat from hell. I hope it is audible," Wilner told Drexel TV's Paula Cohen Martinez. Wilner was about to read a poem from her 2004 collection, *The Girl with Beads in Her Hair*. Wilner's voice, as it turned out, was flawless. Philadelphia's most famous female poet read with tranquil assurance. Later in the show, she would read "On the Road to Larry Robin's Bookstore," a colorful, partially imagined odyssey of traveling through the city to reach the annual celebration of 100 Poets, at Robins' Bookstore (now Moonstone) Poetry Ink. Part Dante's *Divine Comedy*, part Ginsbergian circus, the poem weaves in and out of the city's back alleys and streets, bars, houses and more until the bookstore is in plain sight. "Nowhere else in Philly," Wilner has written about the 100 Poets event, "do we get such a wonderful mix of people, voices, and of generations, and it is an experience in the varieties of personalities as much as in poetry and poetics." Wilner breaks down Poetry Ink as containing everything from "uplift to satire, political protest to personal sorrow, love poems and tirades, transgression and decorum, the outrageous and the outraged, ranters and restrained formalists, street and academy, performance poets and shy ladies barely audible—pretty much the human spectrum."[75]

Born in 1937 in Cleveland, Ohio, to Bernard Everett, a lawyer, and Gertrude Rand, an artist, Wilner obtained a BA at Goucher College, Maryland, in 1959. After graduation, she worked as a reporter for the *Baltimore News American* and then went on to get a master's and then a PhD from Johns Hopkins University. Her Johns Hopkins thesis was published in 1973 under the title *Gathering the Winds: Visionary Imagination and Radical Transformation of Self and Society*. After her job at the *News American*, she did not continue in journalism but taught English at Morgan State University. Like many poets born in other parts of the country, she found her way to Philadelphia, where she became editor of the *American Poetry Review* from 1975 to 1977. Wilner's first book of poetry, *Maya* (University of Massachusetts Press, 1979), was published when she was forty-two years old. The fact that she came relatively late to poetry has not hurt her poetic output. Wilner has not had to disown anything she wrote in her twenties, an act that sometimes occurs with writers who publish too young. New York–based writer Fran Lebowitz, for instance, has written that she finds little to compel her to read the work of writers in their early twenties. "I don't know why people are interested in them," she said. "Do I expect to meet a 22 year old who knows more things than I do? No. I would like to meet a 64 year old. I like to have conversations up, not down."

In Wilner's world, the reader often hears women's voices. Often these are biblical or mythic women who, although they may appear to be minor characters in scripture or classical text, come alive in a major way when they become part of a Wilner work. In her third poetry collection, for

This page: Paul Robeson posed for artist Antonio Salemme sometime in 1929 or 1930. Salemme's fifteen-foot-high nude statue became world famous, but its showing in Philadelphia was halted by the Philadelphia Art Alliance. Salemme's statue of Robeson was later honored by Mayor Wilson Goode in a ceremony organized by Moonstone, Inc. *Courtesy of Larry Robin.*

Antonio Salemme. *Courtesy of Larry Robin.*

instance, the 1989 *Sarah's Choice*, the reader enters the world of the Old Testament, but with a Wilner twist. In Wilner's rendition of the story of Isaac and Abraham, God does an about-face and doesn't speak to Abraham first but comes to Sarah, ordering her to do the unthinkable: sacrifice her son. Sarah, no wilting flower, is not about to go gentle into that good night:

> *"No," said Sarah to the Voice.*
> *"I will not be chosen. Nor shall my son—*
> *if I can help it. You have promised Abraham,*
> *through this boy, a great nation. So either*
> *this sacrifice is a sham, or else it is a sin.*

Shame," she said, for such is the presumption
of mothers, "for thinking me a fool,
for asking such a thing. You must have known
I would choose Isaac. What use have I
for History—an arrow already bent when it is fired from the bow?"

Wilner says that she has always thought of the empty page "not as a surface on which to write but as a place to enter, an elsewhere which the imagination opens to us." She believes that the computer has made this space palpable and believes it is good for readers "to think of their poems less as journal pages and more as another space where vision can occur."[76]

Her many prizes include the Juniper Prize for Poetry, the Pushcart Prize and the Warren Fine Poetry Prize. The Mac Arthur Foundation fellow (1991–96) is also a serious civil rights and peace activist who doesn't hesitate to touch on politics in her work. Although Wilner rarely uses the word "I" in her poems, she agrees that there are some great confessional lyric verses. A good example of a Wilner confessional "I" poem is this verse from her collection *Mine Eyes Have Seen the Glory of...*:

I have grown tired of keeping your accounts,
shaping a story from the chaos of your caprice,
the endless invention of your unconcern; I tire
of the argument, the contention, the attempt
to make a plot out of quicksand and fog,
to rouse the wind when becalmed, to comfort
the dead with a song.

Wilner, who lives in the city's Antique Row neighborhood of Pine Street, married physics professor Robert Weinberg and has one daughter, Trudy. She is also the author of *Otherwise* (University of Chicago Press, 1993); *Reversing the Spell: New and Selected Poems* (Copper Canyon Press, 1998); *Precessional* (ELM Press); and *Tourist in Hell* (University of Chicago Press, 2010).

PHILADELPHIA'S ROSENBACH MUSEUM AND LIBRARY might be called the city's poetry museum, especially considering the museum's 2013 "romance tour," which was based on the museum's collection of manuscripts, books and personal artifacts of some noteworthy poets and writers.

The life of poetry came alive at the Rosenbach when visitors were able to open a window into the love life, poems and letters of Lord Byron, Robert Burns, Charles Dickens, James Joyce, John Keats and Oscar Wilde.

Visitors learned that Charles Dickens was so in love with his wife that at her death, he took off one of her rings and wore it for the rest of his life. After that, his only wish was to be buried with her and to have his ashes mingle with hers. Dickens, who never missed a newspaper deadline in his life, missed his first deadline at her death. That famous Rosenbach exhibit also included a lock of Dickens's hair.

The Rosenbach display included the last love letter poet John Keats wrote to the love of his life, Fanny Brawne. Keats was a painfully shy guy who felt uncomfortable around women and who, at times, was even contemptuous of them. In 1818, the young poet confessed, "I am certain I have not a right feeling towards Women—at this moment I am striving to be just to them but I cannot—Is it because they fall so far beneath my Boyish imagination?"

Unfortunately, during the Victorian era, romantic love was so highly idealized that most men (and women) probably felt that their feelings for a loved one could never match the "heavenly" ideal.

"I hope I shall never marry," Keats also wrote, "as my solitude is sublime."

Because he was too poor to support a wife, Keats never married. His love letters to Fanny are also filled with a painful mix of love, joy and images of death.

When Keats died at the tender age of twenty-five, still relatively unknown as an artist (this would change after his death), Fanny married but kept her relationship with Keats a secret. Later, as Keats's work became well known, she told her children about the love affair and even showed them Keats's letters to her. She made her children swear not to spill the beans to their father. After Fanny's and her husband's deaths, the eldest son, Herbert, sold his mother's letters for a tidy sum. This untoward transaction caused a scandal, a fact not lost on Oscar Wilde, who wrote a poem, "Love for Sale," which was on display at the Rosenbach.

Visitors to the museum learned that English poet Robert Burns sired eight illegitimate children and nine legitimate children and had so many affairs with women in his hometown that it aroused the ire of neighbors. Burns was a masterful con man when it came to love: on display was a love letter he wrote to one girl he described as "the sweetest love he ever had." Perhaps no one knows how Burns was able to manage to distinguish one love among so many as "the sweetest."

Yet no poet "kicked" love around like Lord Byron. This handsome, rich, bisexual aristocrat was the rock star of his time.

On display at the Rosenbach is the manuscript of his poem "Prometheus," as well as the poet's leather card-carrying case, which he used to distribute his cards to numerous stalking, breathy ladies and perhaps men as well.

So popular was Byron that when he married AnnaBelle Milbank, he did not get married in a church but had to get married at Annabel's parents' house because there were too many groupies and wild people clamoring to get close.

Philadelphia's most famous cultural observer, writer Camille Pagila, author of the classic *Sexual Personae*, writes that "poetry began in ancient ritual as rhythmic chanting, and its early history was intertwined with music and dance. It belonged to the oral tradition for millennia until the invention of writing. After that, the visual format of the poem on the page became intrinsic to its identity."[77]

Two classic poets who were educated in Philadelphia but then went on to move to other cities were Hilda Doolittle, or H.D., and Marianne Moore.

Early photographs of the poet Hilda Doolittle show an elegant young woman who, in many ways, resembled actress Glenda Jackson in Ken Russell's 1989 film *Women in Love*.

Born in 1886 in Bethlehem, Pennsylvania, to a father who was a University of Pennsylvania astronomy professor and a mother who was a pious Moravian, Doolittle at age fifteen was, according to poet William Carlos Williams, "tall, blond, with a long jaw and gay blue eyes."

In 1895, the family moved to Upper Darby, Pennsylvania, where her mother's religious beliefs (in Moravian theology, all souls are female and Christ is the husband of the male as well as of the female) began to form the foundation of young Hilda's growing poetic consciousness and eventual attraction to ancient Greek culture.

In 1901, at a Halloween party on the Penn campus, she met poet Ezra Pound, then a handsome, muscular undergraduate. Their relationship and eventual engagement flourished during Doolittle's two-year tenure at Bryn Mawr College, until Pound abruptly ended the romance.

Doolittle later followed Pound first to New York and then to London, where she agreed to meet him on the steps of the British Museum in order to show him samples of her poetry. Pound admired the brevity and easy rhythm of Doolittle's verse and helped launch her career as a poet.

In his amusing but cryptic essay on Doolittle in *Prophets and Professors*, Bruce Bawer asks how Pound could build poetry reform with imagism around the works of a poet named Hilda Doolittle: "So, before Pound tipped his hat and departed…that day, he scrawled something at the bottom of the manuscript of Hermes; H.D. Imagiste, Voila!' The pathetic, pretentious and much-patronized Hilda was no more."

But Pound abandoned H.D. again—this time as a poet and not a lover—when another poetic school (vorticism) caught his eye.

By this time, Doolittle, as H.D., was already published in Harriet Monroe's *Poetry* magazine and in *Des Imagistes*, the 1914 anthology of imagist poets.

Though intimate relationships between women were commonplace early in the twentieth century, women with lesbian inclinations were categorized as spinsters or pressured into heterosexual marriages. As a result, many women's self-awareness of lesbian feelings usually occurred later in life. Doolittle's own "discovery" was not actualized until after her 1913 marriage to poet Richard Aldington, which lasted several years.

In the 1920s, Doolittle met writer/filmmaker Winifred Ellerman, who used the pseudonym Bryher. One of the richest women in England, Bryher supported Doolittle and provided her with a comfortable life so she could write.

The relationship between Bryher and Doolittle was more of a business relationship than a "marriage," but Bryher's love and commitment to Doolittle was the driving force behind a union that lasted forty years.[78] Bryher published several of Doolittle's books, including her 1926 autobiographical novel, *Palimpsest*.

Though her novels were panned by critics as "slack and indulgent," Doolittle's work attracted the attention of T.S. Eliot and D.H. Lawrence. Her collected poems include: *Hymen* (1921), *Heliodoroa* (1924) and *Red Roses for Bronze* (1929).

Doolittle chose not to publish her explicitly lesbian works during her lifetime. "Pilate's Wife," "Asphodel" and "Hermione" were published after her death in 1961.

In the Rosenbach Museum, you will also find poet Marianne Moore's Greenwich Village living room preserved in its original layout. Here, one can imagine what it must have been like when Moore, a friend of Ezra Pound, William Carlos Williams and T.S. Eliot, began her routine of doing chin-ups.

Visit the Moore Room at the Rosenbach and you will see the metal chin-up bar in the poet's reconstructed living room. You'll also spot a nineteenth-century settee and bureau, a footstool (a gift from T.S. Eliot) and a painting of a yellow rose by e.e. cummings.

Personal belongings aside, the details of Moore's life remain as obscure as some of the meanings of her rhyming syllabic verse, which the *Cambridge Guide to Literature* calls "marked by an unconventional but disciplined use of metrics, and a witty, often ironic tone." Nowhere in the *Cambridge Guide*—or in Helen Vendler's 528-page critique of American poets, *Voices and Visions*—is anything stated about Moore's romantic life. What we do know is that she was born in 1887 near Kirkwood, Missouri, and that she lived with her maternal grandfather, John Warner Moore, who became an ordained minister in 1914. The family then moved to Carlisle and, in 1916, to Chatham, New Jersey.

After graduating from Bryn Mawr, a publisher told the young poet she should forget poetry and become a secretary. Moore followed the publisher's advice for four years, though one of her works was published in Harriet Monroe's *Poetry* magazine. Additional poems were published in *Others* magazine. According to Vendler, these early poems echoed Moore's concern that each work be part of a continuing effort to think through what poetry is. Though Moore would always examine painting, sculpture and decorative arts in her work—what Pound called "the logic of juxtaposition"—Vendler said that Moore's way of writing became a search for identity. Moore herself called most poetry "prose with a heightened consciousness."

During most of her career, Moore condemned free verse, saying "it was the easiest thing in the world to create, with one intonation in the image of the other."

In 1918, she moved with her mother to a basement apartment in St. Luke's Place in Greenwich Village. The move was beneficial, since Moore believed that living in the city offered an "accessibility to experiences." New York also radically expanded her ideas about poetry. What once had been a search for personal identity—she believed in Emerson's dictum that "artistic imitation is suicide"—was transformed into a fascination for the world of trade and commerce. Because of commerce, Moore came to respect the values and inevitability of "influences." T.S. Eliot's collection of essays, *Sacred Wood*, also helped her see the value in the existing monuments of the past.

Her first book of poems was published in 1921 and her second, *Observations*, in 1924. In 1921, she began to write free verse, and in 1926, she became editor of the prestigious literary magazine the *Dial*. Her *Collected Poems* (1951) received the National Book Award and the Pulitzer Prize.

In her poem "Marriage," Moore writes:

> *This institution,*
> *perhaps one should say enterprise*
> *out of respect for which*
> *one says one need not change one's mind*
> *about a thing one has believed in,*

requiring public promises
of one's intention
to fulfil a private obligation:
I wonder what Adam and Eve
think of it by this time,
this fire-gilt steel
alive with goldenness;
how bright it shows—
"Of circular traditions and impostures,
committing many spoils,"
requiring all one's criminal ingenuity
to avoid!

Throughout her life, Moore was a conservative Republican. She even voted for Herbert Hoover.

Before her death in 1972, Moore willed her literary and personal papers, as well as the contents of her living room, to the Rosenbach.

Since new and interesting writers can appear at any time, literary Philadelphia is not a locked-in world. This is true even if certain reading venues in the city tend to cultivate certain types of writers to the exclusion of others. What this means, of course, is that some good writers are left out of the programming. In 2013, the city, in partnership with the Free Library of Philadelphia, arranged "Philadelphia's Literary Legacy: Selected Authors, Playwrights and Poets—from Writers of the Declaration of Independence to Present Day," at Philadelphia International Airport. City librarians were assigned the task of selecting the featured scribes based on whether the writers had ever had a bestseller or had won a prestigious award, like a Nobel or a Pulitzer Prize for Literature. Although criteria of this sort can severely (and unfairly) limit the names of living writers, the exhibit successfully showcased most of the important writers from the city's past, such as George Lippard and Agnes Repplier. It was especially gratifying to see that Repplier had made the airport "runway" grade.

Exclusion from "coveted" literary lists, exhibits or anthologies does not imply a *hurt* talent in need of improvement. While a book like *Literary Philadelphia* cannot include every working (talented) writer in the city, it can certainly set the stage for a wider canvas in the future. The lyric and narrative poetry of South Philadelphia's Ryan Eckes comes to mind, as does the work of more standard-bearer scribes like W.E.B. DuBois, Noam Chomsky and Margaret Mead. The work of Ken Kalfus, Lisa Scottoline, Jennifer Weiner, Jon McGoran and Simone Zelitch also demands attention.

NOTES

Chapter I

1. Richard Godbeer, *Sexual Revolution in Early America* (n.p.: L JHU Press, 2009), 299.
2. Ibid.
3. *William and Mary Quarterly* 63, no. 4.
4. William Penn, *The Fruits of Solitude* (Cambridge: The Harvard Classics, 1909–14), http://www.bartleby.com/1/3/115.html.
5. Steven Wells, "Bring the Paine!" *Philadelphia Weekly*, February 8, 2006, http://www.philadelphiaweekly.com/news-and-opinion/cover-story/bring_the_paine-38411579.html.
6. Bertrand Russell, "Why I Am Not a Christian, Our Sexual Ethics, Freedom and the Colleges," excerpted from the paper, http://www.thirdworldtraveler.com/Bertrand_Russell/Fate_Thomas_Paine_WIANAC.html (accessed February 2015).
7. Martin Kelly, "Benjamin Franklin Biography," About Education, http://americanhistory.about.com/od/colonialamerica/p/bio_franklin.htm (accessed April 2015).
8. Robert Sattlemeyer, "Civil War Times," American History Through Literature, http://www.historynet.com/louisa-may-alcott (accessed May 10, 2015).
9. Louisa May Alcott, Project Gutenberg EBook of *Hospital Sketches*, posted March 6, 2009, from James Redpath, Publisher, 1863, http://www.gutenberg.org/files/3837/3837-h/3837-h.htm.

CHAPTER II

10. Edward Pettit, "Monks, Devils and Quakers: The Lurid Life and Times of Lippard, Philadelphia's Original Best-Selling Author," *Philadelphia City Paper*, n.d., http://citypaper.net/article.php?Monks-Devils-and-Quakers-22485.

11. George Lippard, *The Killers: A Narrative of Real Life in Philadelphia* (Philadelphia: University of Pennsylvania Press. 2014), 69.

12. Ibid.

13. "Edgar Allan Poe and Religion," Edgar Allan Poe Society of Baltimore, January 2014, http://www.eapoe.org/geninfo/poerelig.htm.

14. Ibid.

15. Ibid.

16. Mark E. Dixon, "Was Bayard Taylor America's First Gay Novelist?" *Main Line Today*, 2014, http://www.mainlinetoday.com/Main-Line-Today/August-2014/Was-Bayard-Taylor-Americas-First-Gay-Novelist.

17. Ibid.

18. Dan Rattiner, "Tarred and Feathered: Walt Whitman Teaches in Southold," 2014, http://www.danspapers.com/2014/07/tarred-and-feathered-walt-whitman-teaches-in-southold.

19. Ibid.

20. Daniel Mark Epstein, *Lincoln and Whitman: Parallel Lives in Civil War Washington* (New York: Ballantine Books, 2004), 179.

21. Charley Shively, *Calamus Lovers: Walt Whitman's Working Class Camerados* (San Francisco: Gay Sunshine Press, 1987), 25, 27.

22. Muriel Spark, *The Informed Air* (New York: New Directions, 2014), 77.

23. Michael S. Kimmel, *The History of Men: Essays on the History of American and British Masculinities* (New York: State University of New York Press, 2005), 19.

24. Weir S. Mitchell, *Wear and Tear; or Hints for the Overworked* (n.p.: Classics in Gender Studies, AltaMirs Press, 2004).

25. Ibid.

26. Ibid.

27. Anne Stiles, "The Rest Cure," http://www.branchcollective.org/?ps_articles=anne-stiles-the-rest-cure-1873-1925.

28. Kimmel, *History of Men*.

29. Raven Grimassi, *Charles Godfrey Leland: A Biography* (n.p., 2008), available online at http://www.stregheria.com/leland.htm.

30. Charles Godfrey Leland, *Memoirs* (London: William Heinemann, 1894), available online at http://www.amazon.com/Memoirs-Charles-Godfrey-Leland-ebook/dp/B004TOVAXO/ref=sr_1_9?s=b

ooks&ie=UTF8&qid=1433613929&sr=1-9&keywords=charles+godf
rey+leland&pebp=1433614032067&perid=12TC6GD2KDAGT0X4
MX55.

31. Ibid.

32. Charles Godfrey Leland, *Life of Abraham Lincoln* (London: Marcus Ward Co., 1879), 25, 26.

33. Leland, *Memoirs.*

34. George Stewart Stokes, *Agnes Repplier, Lady of Letters* (Philadelphia: University of Pennsylvania Press/Oxford University, 1949).

35. Ibid.

36. Ibid.

37. Ibid.

38. Ibid.

39. Emma Repplier, *Agnes Repplier: A Memoir* (Philadelphia: Dorrance, 1957).

40. John T. McIntyre, *Steps Going Down* (New York: Farrar & Rinehart, 1936), 411.

41. Ibid.

42. Richard Powell, *The Philadelphian* (New York: Charles Scribner's & Son's, 1956), "About the Author."

43. Ibid., 37.

44. Ibid., 38.

CHAPTER III

45. Lawrence Grobel, *Talking with Michener* (n.p.: University Press of Mississippi, 1999), 8, 9.

46. Stephen J. May, *Michener: A Writer's Journey* (n.p.: University of Oklahoma Press, 2005), 73, 74.

47. Grobel, *Talking with Michener*, 2, 3.

48. Christopher Isherwood, *Diaries*, vol. 1, *1939–1960* (London: Methuen London, 1996), 182, 183.

49. Daneil P. Mannix, *My Life with All Creatures Great and Small* (Portland, OR: eNet Press Inc. 1963), 224, 226.

50. Daniel P. Mannix and Malcolm Cowley, *Black Cargoes: A History of the Atlantic Slave Trade, 1518–1865* (Portland, OR: eNet Press, Inc., 1962).

51. Andre Bernard, ed., *Rotten Rejections* (New York: Pushcart Press, 1990), 30.

52. Ibid., 37.

53. Ibid., 34.

54. Peter Conn, *Pearl S. Buck: A Cultural Biography* (Cambridge, UK: Press Syndicate of the University of Cambridge, 1996), Preface.

55. Jesse Pearson and Kyle Johnson, "Pete Dexter interview," VICE, 2009, http://www.vice.com/read/pete-dexter-276-v16n12.

56. Ibid.

57. Ibid.; Ellis E. Conklin, "Let It Bleed," interview, *Village Voice*, 2011, http://www.villagevoice.com/news/let-it-bleed-6433356.

58. Conklin, "Let It Bleed."

59. Ibid.

60. Buzz Bissinger, "My Gucci Addiction," *GQ*, 2013, http://www.gq.com/news-politics/newsmakers/201304/buzz-bissinger-shopaholic-gucci-addiction.

61. Ibid.

62. Ibid.

63. Stephan Salisbury, "Edward Sozanski, Chronicler of the Region's Art," *Philadelphia Inquirer*, 2014, https://www.google.com/?gws_rd=ssl#q=edward+sozanski+obituary+stephan+salisbury.

64. Edward Sozanski, "What Albert C. Barnes Definitely Did Not Want," *Philadelphia Inquirer*, 2012, http://articles.philly.com/2012-05-28/news/31868937_1_barnes-collection-matisse-barnes-foundation.

65. Bob Ingram, "A Call from Allen Ginsberg," *Broad Street Review*, 2014, http://www.broadstreetreview.com/music-opera/a-call-from-allen-ginsberg.

66. Dan Rottenberg, *Death of a Gunfighter* (n.p.: Westholme Publishing, 2008).

67. Dan Rottenberg, *The Outsider: Albert M. Greenfield and the Fall of the Protestant Establishment* (Philadelphia: Temple University Press), 10.

Chapter IV

68. Sonia Sanchez, Oral History Archives, National Visionary Project, http://www.visionaryproject.org/sanchezsonia.

69. CA Conrad, *Deviant Propulsion* (Brooklyn: Soft Skull Press, 2005), "About the Author."

70. Daisy Fried, *My Brother Is Getting Arrested Again* (Pittsburgh: University of Pittsburgh Press, n.d.), book jacket, https://www.upress.pitt.edu/BookDetails.aspx?bookId=35787.

71. Drexel University, "Daniel Hoffman, 14.29," YouTube video, June 05, 2011, https://www.youtube.com/watch?v=tVk0d0UmNtk.

72. Drexel University, "Daniel Hoffman, 13.26," YouTube video, June 05, 2011, https://www.youtube.com/watch?v=kB2v1_C4O4U.

73. Daniel Abdal Havy Moore, "Zen Recollections," Crooked Cucumber Archives, https://www.youtube.com/watch?v=kB2v1_C4O4U.

74. Ibid.

75. Drexel University, "Eleanor Wilner, 14.59," YouTube video, June 05, 2011, https://www.youtube.com/watch?v=B7A4z2XwOBE.

76. Drexel University, "Eleanor Wilner, 13.26," YouTube video, June 05, 2011, https://www.youtube.com/watch?v=7Jf6xRb9SqQ.

77. Camille Paglia, *Sexual Personae* (New York: Vintage Books, 1991).

78. Guest, Barbara. *Herself Defined: The Poet H.D. and Her World* (New York: Doubleday, 1984).

SELECTED BIBLIOGRAPHY

Bawer, Bruce. *Prophets and Professors: Essays on the Lives and Works of Modern Poets*. Ashland, OR: Story Line Press, 1995.

Campbell, James. *Recovering Benjamin Franklin: An Exploration of a Life of Science and Service*. N.p.: Open Court, 1999.

Chatwin, Bruce. *Under the Sun: The Letters of Bruce Chatwin*. New York: Penguin Books, 2011.

Damascene, Hieromonk. *Father Seraphim Rose*. Platina: St. Herman of Alaska Brotherhood, 2003.

Dunlap, William. *Memoirs of Charles Brockden Brown, the American Novelist*. London: Colburn and Co., 1822.

Jennings, Francis. *Benjamin Franklin, Politician: The Mask and the Man*. New York: W.W. Norton & Company, Inc., 1996.

Lukacs, John. *American Austen: The Forgotten Writings of Agnes Repplier*. Wilmington, DE: ISI Books, 2009.

Sontag, Susan. *Conversations with Susan Sontag*. Jackson: University Press of Mississippi, 1995.

Van Allen, Elizabeth J. *James Whitcomb Riley: A Life*. Indiana, October 22, 1999.

Van Doren, Carl. *Benjamin Franklin*. New York: Penguin, 1991.

Vendler, Helen. *Voices & Visions*. New York: Random House, 1987.

INDEX